A GOOD SAMARITAN

A GOOD SAMARITAN

The Autobiography of the Reverend
CYRIL HANDEL GRANT MBE BD STM

SilverWood

Published in 2013 by the author
using SilverWood Books Empowered Publishing®

SilverWood Books Ltd
30 Queen Charlotte Street, Bristol, BS1 4HJ
www.silverwoodbooks.co.uk

ISBN 978-1-78132-134-8

British Library Cataloguing in Publication Data
A CIP catalogue record for this book is available from the British Library

Set in Garamond by SilverWood Books Ltd
Printed by Berforts on responsibly sourced paper

Contents

Foreword

By Mary, Lady Fuller

There can be few more unusual chance encounters than the one I had with a person some forty to fifty years ago, when he just happened to be on a boat crossing the Sea of Galilee. Cyril Grant was taking a party of tourists from Redland Park Church, Bristol, and this was the latest in a series of visits he had made to the Holy Land.

I was also visiting the area with a party from Swindon, and had developed a very nasty and contagious cold, accompanied by a hacking cough. Another of the Bristol party, Hedley Funnell, seeing my situation, persuaded me to take some cough sweets he had in his pocket and by the following day I was fit and well; well enough, in fact, to make conversation with Cyril and Hedley as we headed over to visit a kibbutz.

We came to know each other very well and while there are few of us left, Cyril and I retain a friendship which has endured over the years.

Introduction

By John Funnell

In 1962 I was to meet Cyril Grant for the first time as he came to my parents' home in Clifton, Bristol. At the age of seventeen I was impressed by his magnificent beard as well as his amazing presence; little was I to know that he would become a very dear friend over the future passing years.

My father, Hedley, was a Quaker and met Cyril when he became their representative on the board of an ecumenical magazine called *Contact*. Cyril represented the Congregational Church and they quickly established a close friendship enhanced by their mutual love of music. Cyril's taste in classical music covered all sorts of little known composers and our house became the place where his tastes were shared by the neighbourhood as Hedley had a real passion for his hi-fi.

Many years passed before my path crossed with Cyril's again and this was when I was to marry in 1967 Veronica, mother of three of my children, in a double wedding with my sister and her husband-to-be James.

Cyril's friendship was such that when my marriage came apart, it was he that I turned to for advice and comfort as I was living in Bristol at the time and he was most understanding, impartial and non-judgemental (important qualities in a Samaritan!). He married me again to my second wife Gay at his church in Redland in 1979.

In 1988 I had a near-fatal car accident which left me with brain damage and certain other impairments but when Dolores, Cyril's wife of nearly sixty years, died, my own mother, who had remained a close friend of them both, helped me to realise that I could do something to help Cyril. By collecting all of his writings from his remarkable life and trying to create his autobiography it would give him a new purpose in life; this was started in 2007 and we eventually got to a point where we realised that we needed some professional help if it were to be achieved.

At this point I knew that we would need a sponsor as I had no funds after my accident. This is where another of Cyril and my mother's close friends was to come to the rescue – in Mary, Lady Fuller, without whom this autobiography would never have seen the light of day.

Chapter One

Beginnings

When I look back on my life – which has been a long one, so I have plenty to look back on – I often marvel at the turns it has taken and the many paths I have walked. I also wonder about the paths I didn't take. From time to time, we all think about 'what might have been', and I know there are certain points in my life when a decision or an occurrence would have taken me into another life altogether.

The first of these happened long before my birth. When my father, William Grant, was a baby he was placed in a high chair for a meal with his parents. During the meal he reached out and grabbed the handle of a teapot full of boiling water and before his parents could stop him, he tipped the whole thing over his head. He was taken immediately to the doctor and his life was saved. Somehow, he managed to escape severe burns but the accident affected him psychologically and for the rest of his life he suffered from tics and twitches.

In 1916 my father was called up for duty in the army. He went for a medical examination, but the panel decided that his twitches and tics rendered him unfit for service. If he'd been passed as A1 he no doubt would have been sent to France, and quite possibly to his death in that horrifying conflict. My mother would've met and married someone else and I would never have been born. So in a strange way, I owe my life to a nasty accident which befell a small child of the Victorian era.

As it was, my parents married in 1917 and I came along on 14 July 1919, in Sparkbrook, Birmingham. None of my names are

English. 'Cyril' is Russian, 'Grant' is Scots and I was given the German middle name of 'Handel' in honour of my father's abiding passion for music. My mother was called Leah Wells, but unfortunately I don't know much about her at all, for reasons I will explain later on. My paternal grandparents originally came from Cheltenham and settled in Birmingham, where my grandfather set up a furniture-making business, WC Grant and Son, the 'son' being my father. In those days furniture was not mass-produced as it is now, so each piece was handmade and both my father and grandfather were experts at creating beautiful, solid furniture. Sadly, perhaps, their talents weren't passed on to me but I do remember spending a lot of time in the workshop, watching them as they worked. I still have some of the furniture they made during that period.

I was an only child. However, when I was about six my parents adopted a little girl, some years younger than me. From what I remember of her, she was a happy child and we got on well with her, but after six months with us she disappeared and I never saw her again. She didn't die, I'm sure of that, but I have no idea where she went or what happened to her. We never spoke of her again, and to this day it remains a complete mystery to me.

I grew up in Sparkbrook, in a late-Victorian house on Stratford Road that had been a Church of England rectory. It was a grand place, very large with spacious rooms and a servants' wing. Not that we had servants. My mother was an excellent cook and made all the meals, though we did have someone in once a week to help with the cleaning. My parents rented the house and almost adjoining was the furniture workshop belonging to WC Grant and Son. So all my father had to do to get to work was walk across the yard. The house had extensive and beautiful gardens, with trees and flower beds, and I spent many happy hours playing in it. I have a photograph of myself and my little friends at my fifth birthday party standing outside the grand entrance to the dining room and looking very pleased with ourselves. I expect it was a treat for the local children to play in such a big garden, as the area of Sparkbrook had many terrace houses. Of course, I was oblivious to the fact that we may have been seen as rather different to the rest of the neighbourhood, but I wouldn't say we were a well off family. We just happened to live in a large and handsome house. I was taken back to Sparkbrook some eighteen months ago and the house has long since been demolished. A bus station stands in its place now, and the whole area is rather run down. I was upset to see how it had declined.

I went to Christ Church school, which was just across the road from my house. From an early age I was interested in drama, and the few school photographs I have show me dressed up to take part in various plays. I was a Red Indian in one, and a Mayor in another. English, writing and drama were my best subjects, but I'm afraid I was rather a dunce at mathematics and arithmetic, and this has stayed with me throughout my life. At school I tried hard to understand it but it just wouldn't go in. It certainly didn't come naturally to me, that's for sure.

Perhaps I was always a performer, and it wasn't just my schoolteachers who noticed it. During the 1920s, probably around 1926, we had an occasional visitor to our house in the form of Canon Stuart Morris. He was head of the Peace Pledge Union, a Christian organisation set up with the aim of preventing another terrible war from happening, and he went around the country making speeches. He stayed with us for two weeks while he made speeches in Birmingham's Bullring about the dangers of letting the country drift into another war. He was obviously an inspiring speaker because he attracted large crowds. One day, while he was staying with us, he returned to our house and, to the amusement of my parents, lifted me on to a table and told me to pretend I was addressing a vast crowd. "Talk about anything that comes into your head," he said, and I did. I thought it was marvellous that he'd asked me to do that and it stuck in my mind. Did I realise then that one day I too would be addressing large congregations? Possibly not, but something was planted from that day forward. My parents were Nonconformist Christians and churchgoers, as many people were in those days, and my father, a talented musician, played the organ in a number of Nonconformist churches. I had religious convictions as a child, but I wouldn't say they were particularly strong; at least it didn't feel that way at the time. But who knows, maybe Canon Morris saw something in me, and had an inkling that one day I may join the ministry?

However, there were to be many changes in my life before that happened, not least the decision to move away from Birmingham when I was eight. My parents had a friend called Sadler Cook, a widower living with his daughter in Bournville. He was the leading tenor in Birmingham Cathedral and I imagine my father got to know him via a mutual interest in music. Anyway, he became a family friend and about two years after he made our acquaintance he informed us that he and his daughter would be moving to Margate to open a guest house. Furthermore, he wondered whether my parents would like to join him in this venture. He'd noticed that my mother was a good cook, and wanted her to do the cooking in the guest house. I don't know what the decision-making process was, but something about the idea must have appealed to my parents and they decided to move away from Birmingham and go in with Sadler Cook.

As you'd imagine, this was a very big step. My father would be leaving the family business and the large rectory would no longer be our home. I would be moving schools and living by the sea. It would be a whole new way of life. So in the early part of 1927 we said our goodbyes to Birmingham and headed for First Avenue, Cliftonville, Margate, where the guest house was situated. The first season must have been very successful, I imagine, because at the end of it my mother persuaded my father to take on a guest house of their own, and he agreed to her request. So we were on the move again, and into a guest house of our own where we provided breakfast, lunch, afternoon tea and a four course dinner for just four guineas a week.

After being in landlocked Birmingham, I very much enjoyed living by the sea. Every day seemed like a holiday. With a friend

I would hide under the planked esplanade that ran along the sands beneath the eighty-foot white cliffs. We would shoot our water pistols through the cracks between the planks at the ladies passing above in their finery, making them suddenly aware that they had become wet in their 'unmentionables'. When we were detected we would run in the opposite direction to our pursuers, and we were never caught!

Sadly, these good times were to come to a sudden and tragic end. One evening, during my parents' first season in their own guest house, my mother went to bed. She woke up in the middle of the night with a terrible headache and, with hardly any warning, died suddenly of a cerebral haemorrhage. She was only in her early thirties, and her death was deeply devastating. With the help of another guest house proprietress, who lent a hand with the cooking, my distraught father managed to keep the guest house going while the current residents finished their holidays, but there were to be no more paying guests after that. As was common then, little attention was paid to the feelings of a child caught up in the aftermath of a parent's death, and I simply had to get on with it. I wasn't allowed to attend my mother's funeral and to this day I don't know where she is buried. She wasn't spoken of much after her death, which is why I don't know an awful lot about her.

I don't know what my father did for work immediately after my mother's death, but I do know that within six months he married again. He was the organist at a church in Margate and it was there that he became friendly with a woman in the choir. Her name was Beatrice, she was a widow with a daughter a little older than me, and she owned a guest house in another part of Cliftonville. She and my father must have hit it off for as I say, they were married quickly. What became clear was that while Beatrice very much wanted my father, she didn't want me. She insisted that I move back to Birmingham and live with my grandparents and my father seemed to have no choice other than to accept this. So while they ran Beatrice's guest house, I was sent back to Sparkbrook and spent two or three years living with my grandparents, who were exceptionally kind people. Goodness knows what they must have thought of their son's new wife and her attitude towards me.

Anyway, a few years passed and somehow or other my father must have persuaded Beatrice that I should return to Margate. Eventually I was sent for, and in 1931 I left Birmingham and my old school once again to re-start life on the south coast. When I returned to Margate my father took me to be interviewed by the headmaster of the local school and I remember being asked by the headmaster to tell him the time from his pocket watch. It showed twenty past twelve, which I said. Then the headmaster asked what it would be if the hands were reversed whereupon I said four o'clock straight away. On hearing this, the headmaster said that they could not afford to do without such a brain in the school and I was offered a place without being asked to take an entry exam!

However, it was obvious Beatrice didn't want me around and deeply resented my presence, because after school was over for the day she dragooned me into all sorts of jobs around the guest house. I cleaned, washed up, prepared vegetables, assisted with the cooking and laundry, and much more. For this, I was given the princely sum of six pence a week, four pence of which Beatrice held back so that she could occasionally buy me socks and underpants. I was a very cheap servant indeed. With my remaining two pence I went to the sweetshop every week and just had enough money to buy five toffees. My father must have seen how humiliating all this was for me, but he wasn't the kind of man to argue with Beatrice and he simply accepted it. Therefore, I had to do the same.

Luckily, I got on very well with Beatrice's daughter, Freda. By the time she was in her teens I had a much better relationship with her than I did with her mother. She eventually married a man in Bristol and had three daughters, Susan, Barbara and Janet, all of whom are still alive. The good relationship I had with Freda carries on with my three stepnieces and I very much cherish them and appreciate their company. As a minister I married them all and they are delightful.

But now I'm getting ahead of myself. Back to the story! The 1930s were, of course, the days of the Great Depression and within a few years of my return the guest house wasn't doing good business at all as visitor numbers dwindled with the economic decline. In 1934 the decision was made to leave Margate and the failing guest house, and move to Bristol, where Beatrice's sister lived. My father was persuaded to take a greengrocer's shop on the Wells Road and, despite knowing nothing about fruit and vegetables, agreed to give it a go. We lived in a flat at the back of the shop, which was somewhat unprofitable. By this time I was fifteen years old and had no real wish to attend yet another school, so I had to look for a job. I bought the Bristol Evening Post and began scanning the employment adverts for something suitable. Quite soon I spotted an advert for a clerk's job at Henry Matthews and Co Ltd, a paint and varnish manufacturers in Lewins Mead in the centre of Bristol. I went along to the interview, with several other boys my age, and I quickly realised that it was a menial office boy's job. Nonetheless, I got the job and was offered a starting wage of 7s 6d a week, which I accepted. No-one was more pleased than my stepmother, who deducted 6s 11d from my weekly wage, leaving me with seven pence. I made a fuss, but she wasn't having any of it and once again I had to accept the situation. By then, my father had a small car and each morning would make journeys to the Bristol fruit and vegetable wholesale market to buy his stock. I got a lift from him every day, but had to catch the tram home in the evening, and so my seven pence didn't stretch very far. Nor did I see many benefits to handing over so much money to my stepmother. Even if I asked politely, I was consistently refused a second helping at mealtimes – a dire situation for a teenage boy! Mind you, this changed when Freda – who by this time was working in a high class ladies gown shop on College Green in Bristol – met a man who worked for an insurance company and quickly fell in love. He was staying in a YMCA and would come to our house every Sunday for a hearty lunch. He enjoyed the food so much that at the end of the meal he said, "Oh Mrs Grant, that was lovely.

May I have a little more?" Well, she could hardly refuse him, and a second helping he was given. I then asked the same question and, with gritted teeth, Beatrice took my plate and gave me some more.

The work at Henry Matthews could be boring, and I knew my heart didn't lie in the manufacturing of paint. In 1934 Lewins Mead was a narrow cobbled gas-lit back street with a variety of small businesses including a rope maker, a packing case maker, a boiled sweet maker, a brewery, and Henry Matthews. The premises and methods of Henry Matthews and Co were almost totally Dickensian with Scrooge-like clerks sitting at high wooden desks scratching away in ledgers with pen and ink. I was expected to be a general 'dog's body' at everyone's beck and call. Our directors were always keen to save money and instead of sending letters through the post to those firms within a mile radius they would send me out with them on foot.

Every afternoon at 3pm it was my job to fetch from Bailey's Café in the Horsefair a pint jug of milk for the office tea, and this chore soon led to a series of events which can only be described as bizarre. It all had to do with the office cashier. He was at the best an eccentric and the worst a madman. Aged about sixty-five, with a violent temper and a drink problem, he kept bottles of beer in his desk drawer and drank copiously from them in the strong room. Toward the end of each office-day he took from an attaché case a large joint of juicy horsemeat, cut it into small pieces on the desk and stuffed them into the pockets of his suit – the one he had worn daily for seven years. At going-home time a dozen cats waited outside the door and followed our cashier up Lewins Mead to the tram stop as he dropped the chunks of meat one by one.

His unpredictable temper made it a daunting experience to ask for petty cash. This he kept in his trouser pocket and upon being asked for a small sum would pull out a fistful of change, fling it all over the floor and snarl, "Take what you want." While pennies, sixpences, shillings and half-crowns rolled in all directions the office staff and I went down on our hands and knees to retrieve it. Once he asked me to buy him a dozen fancy cakes from the Lyons teashop on Wine Street. Then in the office tearoom he asked me to pick out the cake which I judged to be the least attractive in the box. He took a single bite from the cake, handed it back to me and said, "The rest is yours." This became the procedure every Wednesday afternoon for several years.

Nonetheless, the cashier seemed to take a liking to me and one Saturday suggested we went to Bath together on the bus. Before the journey began he insisted upon me turning out my pockets to prove I had no money. Once in Bath my strange companion stopped outside a confectioner's shop, gave me six pence and said, "Go in and get three whipped cream walnuts." When this was done he pointed out a lamp post about thirty yards away and said, "I want you to eat those before we get to that lamp post." I began to think he was not such a bad chap after all. On the same outing a couple of tourists asked for directions to the Pump Rooms, which he gave in the most flamboyant manner, and then bowed low, saying, "Always at your service sirs." It was only then I noticed he had big holes cut into the toe-cap of his boots, presumably to aerate his feet.

This freakish man had no relatives or friends. When he died there were found in his house at Bishopston the mummified bodies of fourteen cats in cardboard boxes, so perhaps he did have friends after all – of a sort.

It was a job, but it wasn't what I wanted. My ambition at that time was to become a journalist. I was keen to write for a living and I could see that being a reporter might be an interesting job. So, in the evenings after work I attended the Merchant Venturers' Technical College, where I studied Maths, French, Typewriting and Shorthand. At eighteen I obtained an RSA certificate for 140 words a minute and became a qualified Pitman's shorthand teacher. This, I thought, would stand me in good stead for my life in the newspaper trade. My ambition was such that I managed to get an interview with AJ Spurll, the then editor of the Bristol Evening Post. During the course of the conversation he asked me what my shorthand speed was.

"One hundred and forty words a minute, sir," I replied proudly. Unfortunately, Mr Spurll looked unimpressed.

"Oh well," he replied, "never mind. You get up to 200 words a minute and you will find that might open doors for you."

And with that, I was summarily dismissed from his office. It was a polite way of saying he didn't want me, because 140 words a minute is perfectly adequate for the purposes of journalism. Two hundred words a minute is almost beyond the bounds of human possibility! I was bitterly disappointed but I didn't let that feeling stay with me, because I had another calling, one that I came to realise would be far more suitable for a person like me. I decided to go into the ministry, and in the next chapter I will explain how this came about.

Chapter Two

Preaching the Word

I've mentioned that we were always a churchgoing family, and this continued when we moved to Bristol. We were regular attendees at Brislington Congregational Church, and worship there was always a great source of comfort to me.

Some time during the mid–1930s, perhaps around 1935 or '36, I was told of an amazing young minister who preached at a Methodist church along the Wells Road, not so far from where we lived. His name was the Reverend R Harvey Field and although young, his reputation had spread far and wide and, according to rumour, people had to queue to get into the church when he was preaching. Well, I had to go and seek out this phenomenon for myself, so one day I went along to the church and squeezed into the packed aisles. There were even people sitting on the pulpit steps. Then the Rev Field spoke, and everything I'd heard about him came true. He had the most wonderful tone of voice, and an unsurpassed way with words. He was someone with an inexplicable aura around him and from that moment on I knew that journalism would come a poor second to a career in the ministry. The experience of seeing this man preach was a turning point, and I knew exactly what I wanted to do with my life.

I knew I'd never be as good as Rev Field, but I had to start somewhere. I got to know Rev Field and he asked me to help out at the church's Sunday school. This I was delighted to do but young though I was, I wanted experience of 'real' preaching. The answer lay in the delightfully named Bristol Congregational Itinerant Society (BCIS), founded in 1811 with the object of 'evangelising the villages in the vicinity of Bristol'.

By the beginning of the nineteenth century, city churches were awake to the need for missionary work in the lands on the verge of being opened up in Britain and other European countries. But there were those even more concerned for people on their own doorstep and they pointed to the 'open wickedness and dense ignorance' that characterised rural life adjacent to the city.

Seventy years earlier John Wesley and George Whitefield found those places to be no less depraved, but as the result of their ministrations many were converted and the scene was transformed, but not everywhere nor perhaps for very long.

Thus in 1808 small groups of Christians from Bristol churches ventured into the outlying communities and during the next thirty years Christian work was begun, or revived, and churches built in sixteen villages within as many miles of Bristol. In nearly every case there first came cottage meetings for prayer and Bible study and the establishment of a 'Preaching Station'. As numbers increased so did the need for a church building, and there are several instances of a plot being given by those sympathetic to the cause.

The first such Christian community to come into being under the auspices of the BCIS was Oldland Common, a village six miles from Bristol, where it is recorded that 'the Lord's Day was an occasion for brutal sports and evil pastimes'. By 1820, a church had been built which could claim to have a congregation of 300 with 120 children in the Sunday school. Preachers walked from Bristol to conduct the services – a round trip of twelve miles; and for the first thirty-six years of the Society's existence there was no transport of any kind.

A hundred or so years later, preachers were still travelling to outlying rural areas to deliver sermons, with varying degrees of success. So, in 1936 and not yet seventeen, I rashly offered my services as a preacher with the BCIS, and was immediately taken on – no questions asked.

In that year, I delivered my first sermon at Warmley, a small cause on the edge of Bristol, dating from 1846. The building, erected for £273, was opened free of debt and, once more, this was due to the generosity of Bristol friends. One of the later members of this church achieved world fame in 1939 when King George VI in his Christmas broadcast quoted lines from a poem of hers published twenty-five years before:

I said to the man who stood at the gate of the year
"Give me a light that I may tread safely into the unknown".
But he replied,
"Go out into the darkness and put your hand into the hand of
God.
That shall be to you better than a light and safer than a known
way".

The author, Minnie Haskins, whose family owned a local pottery and brickworks, had been an ardent worker in the church at Warmley, the Sunday school teacher, as well as leader of the Women's Bible class and the Christian Endeavour.

For the BCIS preachers going out from the city, transport to village churches was always a problem. Long before 1936 however, trains, trams, and cars were in existence, yet even at that time there was no public conveyance in Bristol before 2pm. Therefore, in order to get to my 'preaching station', I had to walk two-and-a-half miles from my home on the outskirts to the city centre street of Old Market. It was here that Mr Pullen of Bluebird Garages in Marshfield waited in a large black Daimler for up to six lay preachers, and there was space in that limousine for more. The vehicle became known to those who rode in it as the 'Hallelujah Chariot', or by some the 'Glory Wagon'.

Mr Pullen would drop us off, one by one, at our various churches along, or adjacent to, the main A420 London road. Warmley would come first, then Wick, followed by Cold Ashton, Marshfield, and finally North Wraxall – fifteen miles from Bristol. Once there, it was for the whole day since all those churches had an evening service, and this always drew a larger congregation. Later in the day it was possible for us to return to Bristol by the hourly bus.

Churches in other directions could be reached by early morning branch line trains. Clutton was on the Bristol to Frome line. The train leaving Temple Meads at 9am was known as the 'Lay Preachers Special'. This was because such people were often the only passengers; they were destined for Congregational, Methodist and Baptist churches at successive villages down the line. Although the line closed in 1964 it lasted longer than some of the churches it served, though little trace of it remains today.

Upton Cheyney, halfway between Bristol and Bath, was one of the remoter outposts of the Society. Situated on the slopes of Lansdown Hill – the site of a fierce battle in 1643 between the forces of Cromwell and King Charles I – its appearance had scarcely changed for hundreds of years. In the 1730s John Cennick, a co-worker with Wesley and Whitefield, came to preach in a farm kitchen. He created such a sensation that hundreds gathered from the surrounding villages hoping to hear him. Before long, however, a gang of hooligans, aided and abetted by the local squire, made trouble by flinging dirt and dead dogs at the preacher as well as whipping him and beating him with sticks. Having heard of this the miners of nearby Kingswood held prayer meetings and public fasts in support of the preacher and peace was eventually restored.

During 1794 an application was made to the Bishop of Gloucester for a licence to hold Nonconformist worship in the village. Eventually a chapel was built in 1834 for £360 and the munificent WD and HO Wills were trustees. In 1849 a day school was added and opened with a class of forty scholars.

As late as the 1930s it was still possible to get within walking distance of Upton Cheyney by taking a train from Temple Meads to Bitton station on the Bristol to Bath, London, Midland and Scottish line. From Bitton the preachers were required to walk the rest of the way along the Bath Road, through the village of Bitton finally turning into a narrow lane that led up to Lansdown Hill.

In 1937 at the time of my first visit, and upon arriving at Bitton station about 10.30am, I realised that it was not going to be possible to get there in time for the eleven o'clock service, but this I was determined to do. Undaunted, I knocked at the door of the only house in the village which had a car parked outside, and explained my predicament, saying that if the owner would drive me to Upton Cheyney I would give him a shilling. (Since my weekly wage was only seven shillings and sixpence this was big money to me.) The owner of the car agreed to my offer even though neither of us knew the exact location of the church. In fact we did not find it. The driver went back home with his shilling and left me to find my own way. After running madly through a ploughed field I arrived drenched in perspiration and full of apologies. Only one person was present – the church secretary. He was quite unperturbed and explained that in order to allow time for the preachers to walk from Bitton, the morning service was not held until 11.30am. Nobody had told me that!

One of my most vivid memories of service with the BCIS in the 1930s and 1940s belongs to Westerleigh. Some eight miles north of Bristol, this church was established in 1815 as a Sunday school. The following year a kindly farmer lent the largest barn in the district for Sunday worship and it became full to overflowing each week. For the next thirty-five years the people suffered from the disability of being without a purpose-built church. No landlord would sell a site because none relished the prospect of having a Nonconformist chapel in the neighbourhood. Eventually a plot was given by a working man, but unfortunately it was well outside the village. As elsewhere, a day school was also started on the premises. Hymns were accompanied by flutes, violins and bass viols.

Then, Westerleigh was well off the beaten track, which may account for some of the eccentricities that characterised people.

One in particular was that at the close of the evening service, before the preacher departed he was asked to wait in the vestry for a few minutes. The deacons then held an impromptu meeting in a corner of the church to decide whether the minister for the day should be given his expenses. If they approved of him he got them; if not, he did not. I might add that there were no women lay preachers in those days.

It was at Westerleigh that I experienced one of the most bizarre Sundays of my life. On 28 August 1940, as usual, hospitality for the day was kindly provided by two elderly maiden ladies. During the afternoon they asked me if I was fond of plums. They had a Victoria plum tree in the garden, which was heavily laden with fruit. I was invited to pick and take home with me as much as I could carry. Encouraged by this I filled two large bags as well as my briefcase. The fruit was so temptingly luscious that I ate more of it than was wise. It was with dismay, therefore, that when being called in for afternoon tea the ladies offered me a huge bowl of plums and custard.

At the 6.30pm service I parked my load of fruit in the vestry and at the close of worship walked with it one and a half miles to the main road hoping to catch the 8pm bus to Bristol. Unfortunately it sped past with a full complement of passengers on board. That meant waiting until 9pm. That one too was packed and did not stop. The 10pm bus was the last, and it took me on board.

Before long we heard sounds of thunder in the distance. But it was not thunder, for Bristol was in the throes of a full-scale air raid. Our driver stopped for a consultation with the passengers. The question was, should we wait outside the city until the air raid was over, or take the risk of going all the way in? We all seemed to be more anxious to get home if possible, in spite of the dangers, rather than sit in the bus – perhaps for most of the night. Consequently we raced into the city, cowering down beneath the seats, and arrived in the centre unscathed, about midnight. Bombs were still being dropped and buildings blazed all around us.

Passengers had to make their own way home as best they could. Our house was on the outskirts, which meant an uphill walk of about two miles, amid thunderous crashes and flames. The journey was made no easier by the fact that I was weighed down by the bags of plums. About halfway, and quite exhausted, I sat down on a roadside seat and ate some of them. At last, sometime in the middle of the night, and with immense relief I arrived home safely to find that my parents were in bed peacefully sleeping and oblivious to the raid. But I was determined they should hear my story, so I woke them up and offered them a plum. They were astonished.

Cold Ashton is a village which, like Upton Cheyney, seemed then to be in a kind of time warp. It was without a Nonconformist church until 1864, and at that time the church at Marshfield, two and a half miles away, was flourishing and its members knew that the people of Cold Ashton longed for services and prayer meetings. A 'scripture-reader' was sent from Marshfield to begin cottage meetings, and soon a chapel was built. For this purpose a local carpenter gave a piece of his own garden, albeit some distance from the village, and adjoining what is now the A46 from Bath to Stroud. In 1880 a Sunday school was established with fifty children.

Cold Ashton was third in line of those dropping-off places between Bristol and North Wraxall. I would arrive about 10am for the 10.30am service. John Lewis, aged ninety, would already be there reading his Bible in preparation for worship. It was the same John Lewis who helped to start the Sunday school in 1880. Being a true countryman he knew nothing of city life and on the few occasions he had been into Bristol, it was always by horse and cart.

He, with wife, daughter, and son-in-law, Mr and Mrs Cainey, would entertain me for the day in their three-hundred-year-old cottage. On one occasion in 1938 there was great excitement because that week they had obtained their first wireless set. It was on all that Sunday afternoon. There was no conversation since all were avidly listening in. Old Mr Lewis frequently broke in with such remarks as, "Wunnerful in it? In it wunnerful?" as though unable to believe his own ears.

Mr Cainey, partially crippled, was almost as old as his father-in-law and appeared to live a separate life from the rest in an adjoining room. On some of my Sunday visits I was invited to spend part of the afternoon with him. This could be a disconcerting experience. He hardly ever spoke and smoked a virulent pipe, which filled the air with its fumes. Instead of joining the rest of us for meals he kept an iron saucepan of thick whiteish-green gruel bubbling away on the coal fire, and every so often would bend forward to lift a ladle of it to his lips. I remember little of what he did say except for one startling statement. It was the early part of the Second World War, soon after there had been an air raid on Bristol. At the end of a protracted silence he calmly remarked, "There be a main big time bomb in the garden." In fact it was so, but none of the family seemed apprehensive. It appears that the bomb went so far down into the ground without exploding that the bomb disposal experts were unable to recover it and as far as I know it remains there to this day.

The church at Cold Ashton received local renown for one eccentricity in its worship. It was this: immediately the Lord's Prayer was announced the members of the congregation (all ten perhaps) would move toward the walls, climb up onto the windowsills and kneel facing outward, resuming their seats at the conclusion of the prayer. No one knows why this was done, but the practice was noted by all visiting lay preachers.

The five years I spent visiting these off-the-wall places and their insular congregations were nothing less than formative. I had a myriad of experiences, some of them rather eccentric, as I've described, but I never had any negative reactions from the people I preached to, and for that I was grateful. I don't think there was anyone as young as me who preached so regularly around the Bristol area and when I look back now I realise the congregations must have been generous in making allowances for my youth. These experiences in the mid to late 1930s more than convinced me that I was 'on the right path', as far as the life of a minister was concerned, and so I now had to give consideration to formal training of some kind. However, there was a rather bigger issue to deal with before I could decide how to proceed with my career. In September 1939 Britain declared war on Germany and, at twenty years old, I was a prime candidate for conscription into the armed services. What was I to do?

Chapter Three

Go West, Young Man, Go West!

From the late 1930s onwards it was obvious that we were on collision course with Nazi Germany. As a teenager this preyed on my mind and, despite the best efforts of those who sought to appease Hitler, I, along with many other boys my age, had a feeling I would be involved in a war sooner or later.

My Christian beliefs told me that it was wrong to kill, no matter how righteous the cause. Therefore, I had no choice other than to become a Conscientious Objector. This was not an easy decision to make, particularly when the Nazis appeared to be threatening the whole of civilisation. The wild scenes and queues outside recruitment offices when World War One broke out were not replicated in September 1939. Instead, there was a quiet resignation that one had to do one's bit. But in my case, that 'bit' could not involve fighting. I told the authorities that I was a Conscientious Objector and I had to appear before a special tribunal which sat to sort out such matters. They tried to persuade me that I was wrong, and that I should be ready to serve in the army, navy or air force. I would not yield, and I felt that even if they didn't agree with my decision, they respected it at least. I just felt that I was destined for something else, and I had to hold on to that conviction.

Besides, it wasn't as if I was wholly refusing to take part in the struggle against Hitler. By 1939 Henry Matthews and Co was involved in the manufacture of blackout paint and so I was included in that work. I also volunteered to go on fire-watching duties at the firm, as it was clear that Bristol would be a major target of the Luftwaffe. And so it came to pass. There were many raids on the city and I shall never forget the crash of bombs dropping and the flames pouring from burning buildings. I was particularly saddened to find out that the Dutch House, a unique landmark in Bristol, had been totally destroyed in one major raid which also wiped out the whole of Castle Street, Bristol's main shopping centre. I passed this building twice a day to and from work. Recently I read of a plan to create the Dutch House once again and I was delighted to hear of such a good idea.

There is no doubt I was in some danger during the fire-watching shifts and I suppose my parents must have been very worried that I wouldn't make it back home. But I was young, and the young don't feel fear like their parents do. When I think back, being in the middle of air raids was terrible but at the time it seemed as if it was something that had been inflicted upon us and there was little we could do about it.

In 1941, on the advice of a friend of my father's, I decided to apply to university as a mature student with the aim of studying for the ministry. I wrote to Lancashire College, an adjunct of Manchester University, and was called for interview. The college was based in Manchester, which at the time was receiving as much punishment from air raids as Bristol, but going up there held no fears for me. On the train up to Manchester I read and re-read the Bible in the knowledge that I'd be asked a lot of questions about it, so by the time I arrived I felt reasonably prepared for what they might throw at me.

The Principal gave me a lengthy interview, during which he asked me what I'd been reading on the journey from Bristol.

"The Bible, sir," I said truthfully. The Principal looked pleased. If only he'd know, that my knowledge of the Holy Book was sketchy, to say the least. Thank goodness I'd made some effort on the train journey up north. The Principal offered me a chance for a year to see how I would make out. I would read Theology and related subjects including Greek and Hebrew.

My parents took my decision to leave Bristol quite well. I expect my stepmother was particularly pleased by the fact I would no longer be asking for second helpings on Sundays! I said my farewells and headed to Manchester for the best part of four years' study.

As this was in wartime the experience of living and studying in Manchester was very spartan; we had a coal fire in the dormitory and discipline was hard. A senior fellow student was appointed Proctor and the Principal would say grace before all the meals. When there were only yesterday's left-overs reheated he would say, "Thank you Lord for these Thy renewed mercies," but if it were not to his liking he would say, "Thank you Lord for this table".

During one period we received rhubarb for every meal as it had prospered in the kitchen garden that year. In spite of our protests it remained on the menu. In desperation we got the cricket roller and flattened the rhubarb into the grass. However, on the next day it appeared again and we discovered the cook had gone out and bought some!

Students were fined if they were not in college by 10.30pm. 10.30 to 11.00pm was two pence, 11.00pm to 11.30pm was four pence, 11.30pm to midnight was six pence. However we found a way in through the coal hole and we all appeared at meals in our gowns. We had our own terms for some of the meals such as 'maggots and varnish' (sponge and treacle) and 'murder on the Alps' (white blancmange with red sauce).

We had living in the college a minister who was Chaplain to the Port of Manchester, the Rev H Roper. I decided to ask him if he would like to come and have a bite with me in my study and he accepted. I was a victim of my own eccentricity and bought for our supper just two pounds of Jerusalem artichokes. I planned to cook them in a saucepan on the coal fire in my study. So far, so good but as they were boiling I thought they would be cooked more quickly if I put a lid on the saucepan. But I did not have one so I put the coal shovel on top of the saucepan. Unfortunately all the coal dust was boiled off the shovel into the artichokes themselves so they looked like coal. Unabashed I took them to the bathroom where I scrubbed each one and proceeded back to my study. The corridor was in pitch darkness and I bumped into a pillar, which nearly knocked me out as well as upsetting the artichokes all over the floor. I gathered them all up and it was then necessary to return to the bathroom to scrub them once again. Eventually they were served up to my astonished visitor who announced that he did not like artichokes so I had to go out and get him some fish and chips.

During the time I was in Manchester I went out to preach in towns and villages within a fifty-mile radius of the city. I was very confident about this side of my ministry training, simply because I'd been doing it for so long in Bristol. However, Manchester was being hit hard by bombing and it wasn't always easy to get back after a service. Quite often I had to find someone to put me up until the following day. I also played the organ at college services, a talent that I inherited directly from my father.

I graduated in the early part of 1945 and I was in the position where I was looking out for a church to settle in. One day I was reading a newspaper and I came across an article about the YMCA looking for volunteers to undertake restoration work in Germany. The war was almost over by then and it was clear that a huge amount of work would be needed to help the defeated nation back on its feet. I felt drawn to this call for volunteers and decided to apply. Shortly after, I received a letter inviting me to come for a medical in London on 8 May. That date wasn't particularly significant on the day it was proposed, but by the time I reached London, to wild scenes of celebration for VE Day, it had taken on a whole new meaning.

I've never seen anything like it before or since. It felt like millions of people were crammed into central London, all celebrating the end of the war against Germany. There were no less than twelve consecutive services at Westminster Abbey alone, and I actually made it to one. There was little chance of obtaining any food, as all the shops seemed to be clean out of everything, though I did manage to get a plate of cold boiled cabbage from somewhere. Finally I made it to the medical examination, fully expecting to receive a clean bill of health.

"I'm sorry," said the examiner when it was over, "but I'm afraid I'm unable to pass you as fit. You won't be able to go to Germany."

"Why not?" I asked, astonished. I'd barely had a day's illness in my life. The medical examiner refused to be drawn any further, and advised me to go home and see my GP. I did this, and the only thing he could detect was a slight increase in my blood pressure, which I immediately put down to the stresses and strains of having to make my way through central London on VE Day! I did appeal to the YMCA in the hope they would reconsider, but they didn't.

As I said at the beginning, I believe that fate, or maybe divine intervention, has played an important role in determining my future. In this case I could have wound up being married to a German *hausfrau* and never been seen again. However fate had a different plan for me. Very shortly after the YMCA episode a lady from America, named Mrs Demarest, arrived at Lancashire College. She was working for the US Committee for War Victims and Reconstruction and after I'd been introduced to her she offered me a travelling fellowship to the US for two or three years in order to continue further study. Well, I was hesitant at first. The United States seemed a terribly long way off and I wondered how I would get on so far away from home. But there was another side of me which was very intrigued by the offer, and when Mrs Demarest said that it wouldn't cost me a penny that clinched the matter.

I was scheduled to sail on the ss *Manchester Shipper* from Ellesmere Port in the Manchester Ship Canal at 7pm on Saturday 24 August 1946. Instructions had previously been received for us to report at the Royal Liver building in Liverpool at 1pm the day before. There we met the Canadian Pacific officials and the immigration authorities and in my case consisted of the one question, "Is your health good?" and the answer, "Yes."

The ss *Manchester Shipper* was one of a fleet of ten belonging to Manchester Liners Ltd. The ships were all cargo boats, ordinarily carrying twelve passengers but converted during wartime to carry seventy-four. And it was seventy-four of us who went aboard that afternoon, graciously ushered into our cabins by a calculating steward whose pantomime of bowing and scraping had something of an oriental touch about it. Six of us had to share a cabin made for two, and when at last we were all in together with our personal luggage we extended our arms (a difficult operation in the confined space) and shook hands all round. Then five of us stood outside while the other had a wash. We were all men, needless to say, but at once saw the necessity for going to bed, getting up, and washing, at different times. My compassion was aroused by the plight of the poor man who slept in the lower birth next to the wash bowl – indeed so close that it might be said almost underneath the wash bowl. His berth was so short that he had either to sleep with his knees up or swing his torso round and down so that his feet rested on the floor, a posture which looked distinctly uncomfortable.

Once embarked, we were not allowed to leave the ship, and the police were posted on the dock to see that no one violated the law. After dinner we amused ourselves by watching the rest of the cargo going aboard. Jet planes in huge crates were swung on to the decks by giant cranes and lashed down by an army of labourers. In the holds were scores of motor cars – part of Britain's export drive – and those who feared for their physical equilibrium on the water hoped that all this weight would keep us from heaving about too much. The total cargo capacity of the ship, however, was 8,000 tons and soon we were to rue the fact that we were not carrying a maximum load.

The passenger list was very cosmopolitan. It included rich South American bankers, war brides, an old bearded French Canadian, a Roman Catholic priest who had been in a Japanese concentration camp for three years; a family of Eurasians who were travelling home from Shanghai after several years of internment, an American oil company official going back to San Francisco from Iran for a six months leave;

a young ex-British army officer going out to teach English at a Canadian high school; and a Mexican family on their way home to Mexico City after having spent four months vacation in England. The largest single group on board was a party of twenty exchange teachers bound for Ontario. All of us were travelling first class priority except one young aristocrat who had been waiting for two years to go to Victoria where he intended to try his hand at apple farming. He had obviously been reading up on Canada and could repeat the most obscure facts with the accuracy of a robot.

At six o'clock next morning in a thick grey drizzle, our physical tie with England was severed at last, and two smoke-belching tugs pulled us very slowly to the mouth of the canal. The difficult business of casting off and getting us through the lock-gate with only six inches to spare on either side, was carried through with perfect precision, and we passed out into the wide and dirty waters of the Mersey. The mists were so thick that for some time it was impossible to see the opposite bank, but as the river narrowed, the Liverpool landscape, dominated by the square tower of the great cathedral, loomed up out of the morning and Birkenhead on the port bow broke into view as a grey mass of unintelligible shapes.

As we passed the waterfront the twin turrets of the Royal Liver building – familiar landmark to thousands of travellers throughout the world – quickly receded into the rain and fog. The river was crowded with traffic from all parts of the world and ships of every nation steamed by in close proximity. When this happens there is always boundless curiosity among crews and passengers alike, and those who can, rush to the deck rail and gaze at their opposite numbers across the water as though other human beings and other ships were things of the utmost mystery and wonder. And so they are; that is what makes it so exciting. And here for a few fleeting moments when we shout to each other, 'good luck' or 'on voyage,' a perfect international relationship of goodwill is established, spontaneous and whole-hearted, unbroken by vetoes or protests. For those who sail the seas there is no barrier of race or colour, and the brotherhood of man reaches its perfect fulfilment.

I had not realised so well before that ships cannot sail where they will, even in wide stretches of apparently deep water. I was amazed to discover how narrow a strip of sea in the broad Mersey estuary is really navigable. A narrow channel of water vividly marked out by black and red buoys every few hundred yards wound out from the Mersey just like a road, and it was along this sea-road, through the maze of buoys and lights, that our pilot gently led us. Presumably we would divert from the crooked but narrow way at our own peril just as a motorist by ignoring the roads signs might run into a ditch. We could see this sea-road twisting and turning about for miles ahead until it was lost in the distance. On either side were shallows and innumerable wrecks. Those below the surface were marked out by lights, but there were many whose masts stood above the water – reminders of the grim fate which befell so many ships when Merseyside was furiously attacked by German bombers in 1940–1941.

At midday the Liverpool pilot was dropped and we proceeded under the ingenuity of our own captain. We had lost the low sandy Lancashire coast some hours before together with the dismal pall of smoke and rain which hung over the river. It seemed as though the sea and sky suddenly became boundless and blue together, for the sun burst from the clouds and changed the aspect of the water completely.

It was not long before there appeared almost simultaneously the Irish coast and the Isle of Man to which the ship passed very near. About three o'clock a little black coaster was sighted freely chugging away in the distance; nobody looked at it especially but it was the last ship we were to see for eight days. A group of us stood in the bow that afternoon and just gazed about across the waters. I settled myself in the very prow of the ship, lifted my head into the oncoming wind and was suffused by a sense of extreme well-being, of power and freedom. The situation was indeed exhilarating – I was on the way to a new life and a new world.

About 6pm somebody pointed to a long indentation on the Irish coast, almost hidden by thick clusters of black cloud. It was Lough Foyle, and Belfast must have been really under the weather. Scotland on the other side appeared to be just as menacing and there was much speculation as to the names of the various promontories and islets that gradually came into view and then receded. The only piece of land upon whose identity we all agreed was the Mull of Kintyre, and in the thickening night it was the last of Europe we saw. According to the officers, the last lighthouse on the Donegal coast was sighted at four o'clock in the morning and we started on our way across 3,000 miles of ocean.

Very soon our little company became divided into two groups – those who were seasick and those who were not. Those who were ill found their time fully occupied and did not need any amusement, while those who were not ill amused themselves by speculating on how long it would be before the people who were ill would be better, and how many would be ill by the next day. This was great fun and some of us achieved a remarkable accuracy in our predictions. The captain, being an expert at this sort of thing, was better than anybody else and besides he had secret information about the weather. Some of the folk at our table were absent for days and at last when the seas subsided a little, one of them in response to the pleadings of the doctor would gingerly make his reappearance in the dining-saloon. As he entered he would stand in the doorway and look wildly about him, then make his way wearily to the table as though he were going down into the jaws of hell. Upon being congratulated by his fellow passengers his morale would receive a momentary fillip, only to crash again almost immediately when the multiple odours of the saloon reached the interior of his stomach and were there worked upon by the gentle heaving of the ship. The patient would then shoot from the table like a rocket to a part of the vessel where the demands of nature could be given unbridled freedom. Others would stick it out a little longer and gradually turn colour from a rosy pink to a dirty greenish yellow. The very brave would sit and eat as much as they could, then after a period of silence and complete immobility – the undoubted signs of an internal struggle – would retire at great speed with an apologetic mumble.

All these goings on made meal times very exciting affairs, that is for the second group who were not ill. The ship's doctor sat at our table and from him we received the latest hot news flashes of how various members of the first group were progressing.

Perhaps one of the main reasons there was sickness on board was because of the quantity and magnificence of the food which graced the table four times a day. Every meal was nothing less than a gargantuan feast. The fruits of the earth were served up with subtlety and distinction for the titillation of our palates – or so it seemed to those of us who had endured the rigorous monotony of a six years war diet in England. This was a typical breakfast menu:

Half a grapefruit
Hot or cold cereal
Kippered herring with butter
Two fried eggs, two rashers of bacon and fried potatoes
Buckwheat cake and syrup
Toast and marmalade
Tea or coffee

A wonderland breakfast it was, and the lunches and dinners were even more extensive than the breakfasts. Nevertheless we sat down and ploughed solidly through the menu, determined to make up a six year leeway and not to miss a single crumb. In addition to breakfast, lunch and dinner we had a sit-down tea each day at 3.15pm, and in between these different meals would often refresh ourselves with a few little snacks at the ship's canteen.

As we sailed north and west, out of the influence of the Gulf Stream, the weather began to get very cold, and it demanded our thickest clothes. Some of the passengers actually took to prancing up and down on the deck, while others played tenniquoits until an immense number of rings were lost over the side and they could play no more. Altogether the time passed very happily – that is for the second group – and at night parties of us would gather in the lounge and exchange stories of our adventurous lives, and other stories too! There were one or two couples of course who, having struck up a transatlantic romance, were not interested in our collective talking and who betook themselves to a sequestrated part of the ship where, with overflowing hearts, they spoke to each other words of tenderness and nonsense.

Sometimes after darkness had fallen I would go out on the ship by myself just to stand and think, and drink in the pure dustless air. To stand on the deck of a ship at the dead of night the in mid-Atlantic is an eerie experience. The black waters of the ocean stretching out on every side, unbroken for hundreds of miles, seemed to draw one almost irresistibly. They are once inviting and repelling. As I leaned over the deck rail my eyes tried in vain to pierce the gloom, but I could penetrate no more than a few yards before the heaving waters and the darkness of the night became swallowed up in each other, and rolled on in impenetrable mystery half way across the world.

As we sailed yet further north, to a point within only a few hundred miles south of Greenland, the fall of darkness each evening brought with it a grand display of the Northern Lights, in all their ghostly splendour. We stood night after night – usually very late – and gazed with fascination upon the mighty screen of the heavens. The sky was lit up from end to end with a maze of gigantic spotlights which every moment were changing direction and colour, from white to pink, from green to yellow, from blue to mauve.

By contrast, a couple of hundred miles off the east coast of Newfoundland we ran into dense fog. This terrified one or two of the passengers, for the ship came to an almost complete standstill and its siren bellowed forth with a deafening roar once every minute. Perhaps the chief reason for extreme caution was the presence of icebergs in that region. Though we could not see them, somewhere behind the fog they were there – just how near nobody knew. No doubt the awful fate of the Titanic, which collided with an iceberg in this particular area, preyed upon many minds. I remember getting up at five o'clock in the morning, when the fog was thick and the temperature was low, and near the hatchway stood an old lady with her hat and coat on and her lifebelt all in readiness. How many hours she had been there no one knew.

We understood from the captain that the area to the north-east of Newfoundland is almost permanently foggy. But as we sailed out of this region there was a treat in store for us and as the fog cleared away the icebergs were revealed. To see them for the first time is a shock to the senses for they are like nothing else on earth. I shall never forget that Thursday when at about 3.30pm I was called out on deck.

The air was clear, whereas a few hours before it had been opaque, and it was now possible to see about twenty miles on every side. Over on the other side of the ship, a couple of miles to the east, there was an enormous iceberg. It was of mighty proportions and rose like a great island out of the sea, towering with a cathedral-like grandeur hundreds of feet into the air. That only one-eighth of the total bulk appeared above the water was a fact difficult to comprehend. But there it was. Groups of us stood upon the deck gazing in wonder as the thing gradually receded into the distance. At the end of an hour it was still visible, and then it slowly drifted into the shadows of the night. It was the first iceberg I ever saw and it brought with it a completely new experience of the rare and beautiful.

During the night we passed through the narrows between Newfoundland and Labrador and in the morning we had our first glimpse of the New World – a faint grey blur on the horizon. It was the province of Quebec and as we steamed our way down the Gulf of St Lawrence the land on both sides disappeared. It was here that we caught a glimpse of flying fish, and the frequent sight of Black

Whales breaking the surface of the sea and spouting great columns of water high into the air captured the interest of the passengers. It was here too that we had to battle our way against the heaviest sea of the voyage. The wind roared through the spars and the rigging and it was possible to lean at an angle of fifty-five degrees without any danger of falling backward. The acrobatic cycle upon which the ship engaged was first of all to rise to the crest of a wave, pause momentarily, and then vibrating from end to end plunge headlong into the trough, shooting up from underneath the bows solid masses of glittering spray. Once again we became divided into two groups, but not for long for we soon came within the protection of Anticosti Island which appeared as a black hump on our port bow. This island is 150 miles long and sixty wide, practically uninhabited except for wild beasts which roam about its thick forests.

The weather now became much warmer for we had been on a south-westerly course for a couple of days. The sun shone from a cloudless sky and the water which had turned from salt to fresh was very calm. Most of the passengers reclined in the bed-chairs and surveyed the landscape as the ship moved upon its way. I remember seeing one of the dignified University of Manchester professors lying out full length on the top of a jet-plane crate. The sun was warm, the breeze gentle, the ship was steady, and idleness was sweet.

About 10pm on Friday night the ship heaved to just off Rimouski to pick up the St Lawrence pilot. Rimouski is a little town of two or three thousand people, but all we could see of it was a mass of twinkling lights. At dawn on Saturday morning the banks of the river were very near and displayed some signs of civilisation. The country was thickly wooded all the way along, but here and there were small clearings and tiny white wooden houses. In the far distance on both sides of the water the dim grey shapes of great mountain ranges could be seen through the morning haze. The first church we saw was on the Isle of Orleans – and like all the rest – it was a small wooden silver-painted structure whose spire gleamed in the sunlight.

All day Saturday the ship slowly threaded its way through a maze of lovely islands which broke up the river into several streams. Gradually the little clusters of white wooden houses which studded the hills at intervals along the route blossomed out into infant townships, and as we penetrated further into the interior of the country the most excited man on board was the old bearded French-Canadian priest. He had been a prisoner of war in Japanese hands for nearly three years and was returning to his native land after being sixteen years away. Nearly all day Saturday and Sunday he was dancing about on the deck, extolling the beauties of Quebec, and delivering an oration to us upon every petty landmark that came into sight – and many that did not – and it was all done with the solemnity of a sacred rite.

Not until we almost reached Quebec City did we see our first ship since leaving the British Isles. It was a small freighter bound for Newcastle upon Tyne. We all crowded to the side and its crew shouted to us, "How is the old country?" to which on the spur of the moment we could find no reply, so we roared back to them a lot of incoherent noises which were at least non-committal.

On the Sunday morning Quebec City appeared on the skyline ahead. The huge *Château Frontenac*, famous as one of the meeting places of Roosevelt and Churchill, and their satellites, dominated the scene from beginning to end. The great pile is built upon the Heights of Abraham up whose precipitous 500 foot cliffs General Wolfe and the British Redcoats scrambled in 1709 in their effort to wrest the domination of Canada from the French. Just how mighty a feat that was, and how foolhardy a project it must have seemed at the time, I did not realise until then. And now nestling under the lee of towering cliffs were dozens of little craft and enormous sextuple-decked ferry boats.

All day on Sunday there was much speculation as to what time we should dock and as Montreal drew near, great activity broke out among the crew and the passengers. Many of the deck-hands were busy oiling the winches, laying out ropes, swabbing the decks, and polishing the brass work. Passengers – especially female ones – spent a deal of time making themselves look as though they had not spent a week in company with heavy seas. They packed suitcases, and settled tips on stewards, waiters and bartenders who took care to make themselves conspicuous during the last few hours.

Up until this time the maple woods and the conifers had grown in thick profusion right up to the water's edge with one or two little towns cut clean out of the forest. But on Sunday afternoon the woodlands disappeared and gave way to urbanisation, and in the distance the semi skyscrapers and chimneys of Canada's greatest city broke into view. We had steamed 900 miles from the open sea.

Within one hour the *Shipper* had turned about almost at right angles and glided slowly into the dock. This was the tense moment for many of those on board who had been away for years, and whose relatives, excited beyond measure, now waited only a few yards away behind the sliding doors of the customs sheds. The waiting friends were hidden from sight and prevented from coming to the ship. Nor were the passengers allowed to disembark until they had complied with immigration formalities. Canadian and USA officers came aboard together with a number of CPR officials who gave individual advice to all passengers about rail travel. Once again, and for the last time, our pleasant little company became divided into two groups – but not on the same basis as before – and this time all of us had to suffer. We were classified according to our destination. Those who were for Canada presented their papers in the dining-saloon, while those bound for the USA, Central and South America had to suffer their torment down in the lounge. And torment it was, for every passport and six pages of visa had to be checked and stamped, special forms had to be made out and signatures had to be obtained for presentation at the frontier – operations which took about ten minutes per person.

The next procedure was to consult with the CPR officials on board about the following stage of the journey. Some of the exchange teachers were bound for Toronto, others for Niagara and still others

45

for tiny settlements in the far north near Hudson Bay. Some of us were faced with the prospect of a train journey of four days for such places as far away as we had already come. Most of the Latin and South American people decided to go to New York and there await transportation by sea or air. The grey, cold and austere climate of immediate post-war England seemed far, far away.

Chapter Four

Waking up to the American Dream

When the ship docked in Montreal, mail was brought aboard and I received a message of welcome from the War Victims and Reconstruction Committee in New York, with instructions to travel down that night to the Madison Square Hotel where accommodation had been reserved. The process of passing the immigration, however, had taken so long that it was quite impossible to leave Montreal that night, and in any case we had not yet experienced the doubtful privilege of passing the customs.

The luggage was swung ashore by crane and the whole dock area was a scene of feverish activity. There seemed to be hundreds of people milling around – immigration and customs officials, ships officers, bus drivers, taxi-men, dockworkers, police, travel agents and distracted passengers who wanted to get away that night – all of them were dashing about and shouting at one another. I eventually had to almost drag an inspector to the scene of my baggage. He took a small peep inside my tiny case and was satisfied. As I wished my trunk to be sent down to New York in advance, arrangements were made for it to be sealed and undergo inspection on my arrival.

We were told it was impossible to find overnight accommodation in Montreal, as the city was full of people who had come to the city for Labour Day celebrations of 3 September. The captain therefore graciously allowed us to stay on board overnight and having thus settled all problems a party of us set out at 9.30pm to see something of Montreal. The city was a blaze of light; hundreds of people were parading in the warm summer air and the shops were crammed with the most luxurious and exotic foods. On the artery of the city – St Catherine's Street – it was with great excitement that we went into a restaurant to eat our first meal on North American soil. Everything inside was new, bright and efficient, and at once we were ushered to our table by a hostess who was the epitome of grace and charm.

When the waitress appeared for the order it was almost impossible to make a decision, and our grappling with the fantastic terminology of the menu left us in a state of indecision. Would we have cherry-stone clams to begin with, or Italian antipasto, or perhaps Beluga Caviar? Then maybe a little Chicken Okra, or Mornay, or Stuffed Olives? On the other hand it might be interesting to try Fried Jumbo Frogs Legs, or Tenderloin Steak Bouquettiere, Pate of Venison or Lobster Thermidor. For the dessert such dishes as Charlotte Russe, Lady Fingers, Frozen Eggnog or Bar le Duc might have some surprises for us. Then, if after all this, we still retained some enthusiasm, we could have some cheese; but we must decide whether it be Camembert, Philadelphia Cream, Cottage, Swiss Gruyere, Liedercranz, Roquefort, Gorgonzola, Imported Swiss or just plain American. But surely it is possible to order a cup of tea? Yes, of course, but only after we decided whether it should be Ceylon, Oolong, Orange Pekoe, Green, Breakfast or Chinese. At last after grave attempts at decoding the menu we got something to eat. Exactly what it was is difficult to know, but to say that we consumed it with relish is something of a feeble understatement.

Next morning we paid our respects to the captain – an old Manchester man whom we had got to know very well – and left our floating home for the last time. The Mexican family and I, together with the others, booked rooms at the Queens Hotel and then started on a sightseeing tour of the city.

Montreal was founded in 1642 by Paul de Chomedy, *Sieur de Maisonneuv* and named after Mount Royal, the mountain which overlooks the city. Then, Greater Montreal covered an area of fifty square miles with a population of one and a half million, two thirds of which was French speaking. This was the largest city in Canada and the third largest French speaking community in the world. It contained nine hundred miles of streets, the finest natural mountain park of any city. It was the largest inland seaport in the world, the home of the world's two largest transportation systems – the Canadian Pacific and the Canadian National – and the only urban centre in North America with complete winter sports facilities. St Catherine's Street West was the Broadway of Montreal and at this geographical centre French and English cultures met. All the signs and advertisements were printed in both languages.

There were two features about Montreal which impressed themselves upon my mind. In order of intensity it was first of all the super abundance of food and its low price. If we had come from a normal Europe this feature would have been surprising enough, but after enduring bread sausages, stodge pudding and powdered milk in England for six years, the fare which graced the shop windows of this city we could hardly believe was anything more than an optical illusion, until we bought some of it and discovered its reality. In England that summer people had queued up to buy peaches at two shillings each; here for sale at every corner they were three pence a pound. Black grapes were selling at a shilling a pound and huge William pears at two pence each. Oyster steaks, champagne, mushrooms, strawberries and so on were all to be bought as articles of every day consumption within the means of ordinary middle class folk. It was indeed an Eldorado and we went about in stupefaction like a lot of poor children let loose in a toy shop. It was with awe, almost a sense of doing something wrong, that we went into shops and bought fruit and chocolates, and ate steaks, or drank iced tomato juice. And then when we could consume no more we just stopped in our tracks before bulging windows and feasted our eyes upon roast turkeys, ducks, hams, shelled nuts, red bananas and Turkish Delight. In this way we staggered about the city, feeling as foreign as though we had arrived from another planet.

Of course the stores which sold non-edible goods displayed just as much variety and abundance as the others but it is difficult to rouse much enthusiasm about a surfeit of lawn mowers, chisels or the chic evening gowns which were no doubt of exceptional quality and style. The second great dent which this city made on my mind was by its plenitude of colour. The women were colourful to the point of gaudiness. They wore flaming hats embellished with brilliant feathers. Their coats and dresses were dazzling. Their fingernails were a bright crimson and the men-folk followed suit but more timidly. Their gorgeous multi-coloured ties were famous and smiled at throughout the world, and nearly every other fellow we saw boasted a straw trilby encircled by a band of wide ribbon by the side of which Joseph's coat would pale into insignificance. I thought quite innocently that one woman who had a black cloak with gold epaulettes was on her way to a fancy dress ball as a cross between Captain Blood and a submarine commander, but I afterwards understood my supposition was mistaken.

Compared with the drabness of England's damaged and unpainted buildings every place seemed to be splendidly bright and in excellent repair. Countless brilliant neon lights, burning thousands of candle power, lit up the streets and turned night into day. Even in normal times I believe there is nothing like it in England, and it seemed to me that no other street could possibly display so much glitter and animation as St Catherine's Street West – but I had yet to see New York!

On the Monday afternoon a party of us from the ship took a thirty mile motor coach tour to an Indian reservation on the other side of the St Lawrence. The river was un-navigable further up than Montreal because of rocky shallows which constitute the Lachine Rapids. These were a wonderful sight and stretched for two or three miles across the river – millions of gallons of water cascading over a confused mass of jagged rocks with the broad expanse of white foam sparkling in the sunlight. Before arriving at the Indian reservation the driver of the coach explained that inside a certain Roman Catholic church, at which we stopped, the priests would conduct a tour and deliver a twenty minute oration on the significance and origin of a few sacred old bones which lay around in glass cases. But no such thing happened, for the priests ensconced in a back room were as busy as cats in a tripe shop selling charms, pictures, rosaries, scented cards, statues and so on. They were of course in extreme good humour and smiled delightedly all the time.

The Indian reservation visit was a failure and a swindle. We saw six phoney-looking Indians on a patch of grass by the side of the road. They too looked very pleased with themselves and were selling so-called Indian souvenirs, such as bracelets and paste jewellery. They also had a food store which did a roaring trade. It was the only one I patronised. Then the six of them got together and did some appallingly puerile dance accompanied by unintelligible and blood-curdling shouts. In between the dances the 'Chief Cofdrop' or 'Big Water' or some such name, cracked feeble music hall jokes, and at the end of it all the party was greeted with the most rapturous applause which was the biggest mystery of the whole show. Upon seeing one of the wretches coming around the crowd with a money box I dashed back to the bus and slammed the door behind me – but was filled with dismay when this same fellow came up and tried to follow into the bus with his moneybox. By the most amazing good fortune I had slammed the door good and hard, so that he was unable to open it. And therefore, sitting in the seat with a smirk on my face and fear in my heart, inwardly anxious but outwardly grinning, I watched his wild wrestling with the door which he kicked and pulled ferociously until he at last confessed defeat and I was saved for posterity. My Indian friend went away with his evil eye gleaming upon me through the window – mine was directed towards his belt in order to ascertain – a purely theoretical question now – if it contained a tomahawk.

The train for New York was due to leave at 8.20am the following morning, which sounds simple enough, but to our uninitiated minds became dreadfully complicated. In the first place, throughout the continent there are five different time zones and after discovering

51

which one we were in, it was found that in this particular zone a state of special 'summer time' existed – not 'double summer time' such as we have in England but 'single summer time'. Then we were told that the railroads took no notice of this artificial time, but operated according to Eastern Standard Time – that is, the majority of the railroads did, but there were exceptions to this general policy. Desperation filled our hearts in trying to work out the time at which the train actually did go. There were heated arguments the night before as to whether we had to arrive at the station an hour before the timetable said the train was due to leave, or an hour afterwards. The consensus was that both courses were far too risky, and that the only way of making sure was to take up a position on the platform three or four hours beforehand.

However, by some trick or coincidence we found ourselves on the New York train at 8.20am which we imagined, by the position of the sun, to be sometime early in the morning. The journey was one of horrible discomfort. With a first class ticket I was pushed with my Scottish and American friends into a dirty coach that was little better than a cattle truck. The seats were like iron benches covered with a piece of thin cloth. The train travelled very slowly and throughout the four hundred miles to New York stopped at every tiny station.

Just before the frontier was reached about noon, as the sixteen coaches crawled on the weary way to the USA, customs and immigration people came and turned us all upside down. They were distantly polite and insisted on seeing everything. The immigration inspector nearly broke my heart. When my papers were asked for I handed over the passport only to be met with a gruff, "Where is the rest of it?" Then it was inevitable – my visa had to go at last. Never in the field of human endeavour has a document, so hard won with tears and sweat, been so lightly snatched away. In order to get it, two special journeys to London were necessary, three interviews with the vice-consul of Bristol, and letters of recommendation and guarantee from different authorities both in England and America. I had been compelled to produce three recent photographs, three birth certificates and information about myself that amounted to a documented life-history in triplicate. The surly inspector did not even look at it and it would have served him right if the whole thing had been out of order. Very soon the six of us went through into the dining car where black attendants in white suits waited upon us with servility. Iced water, iced celery and olives were provided automatically.

In the early afternoon the train began to wend its way fitfully through the Laurentian Mountains and broke out at last on to the shore of the great Lake Champlain across whose sunlit waters there arose the state of Vermont. This was beautiful country, thickly wooded with deciduous trees, and it appeared very like the English Lake District, but on a vaster scale. Periodically throughout the journey attendants came through the car selling fruit, chocolate, milk, sandwiches and cigarettes, and for those who did not wish to pay for such refreshment there was a drinking fountain.

Both the locomotives and the coaches were much larger than their British counterparts. The individual swivel armchairs, with their green velvet, were much more luxurious than anything which could be found in Britain, and the dining cars were reminiscent of pre-war high class English hotels.

At Troy there was no sign of Helen, and it did not look the kind of place her spirit would frequent anyway, yet there was comfort in the fact that the journey was nearly half over. From here all the way down to New York the track ran along upon the north bank of the Hudson River, and the Catskill Mountains over in Pennsylvania were plainly visible. Very soon the famous West Point Military Academy on the opposite bank of the river and the equally famous Sing Sing, which is surrounded on three sides by water, could be seen. At Poughkeepsie we were within ten miles of President Roosevelt's Hyde Park home.

The train drew into New York Central at 8.20pm by my watch – what the real time was nobody knew. Immediately there was a rush for taxis and as we waited a fight started nearby between a taxi driver and a man – had I, I thought, really come to the home of gangsterism?

53

There was no justice or order among the unruly mob of people who stood waiting at the taxi stand. The strongest and the quickest who could rush forward first and grab the handle of the car were the lucky ones. In New York, it seemed, it was survival of the fittest.

All the way to the hotel I saw practically nothing of the city because as there were five of us, and it was illegal to carry more than four, I had to lie nearly full length on the floor of the taxi in case a snooping cop looked in and counted. Accommodation had been reserved at the Madison Square Hotel in Manhattan within the shadow of the then highest building in the world, the 102-storey Empire State Building. So we rested our heads, not yet at our journey's end but within striking distance at last.

When it comes to describing New York, one realises with dismay that even the most hyperbolic words and the most superlative phrases are pitifully inadequate. Nobody can understand the complexity and the contrast of life in this great city without seeing them for himself. Even then, in the immediate post-war era, the glamour and the sordidness, the poverty and the fabulous wealth, the intimacy of its little foreign restaurants and the transcendent grandeur of its slender buildings which rise a thousand feet in the air – were beyond description. It may be understood, therefore, that New York is quite breath-taking – and for a visitor from Europe the speed at which everything moves is doubly confusing, because not only does the traffic travel at a bewildering pace but it all goes on the right-hand side of the street. Always therefore when I stepped off the pavement, in order to see if anything else was coming I would look to the right, and having decided the road was clear, attempt to cross, whereupon I would be nearly bludgeoned to death by a line of traffic bearing down on me from the left.

People of every race, creed and colour struggled together in this crazy metropolis for fame and fortune. It seemed then – and I'm sure it is as true today – that everybody's primary ambition was to achieve a materially comfortable and abundant life – a paradise of cheap self-employment. New York was no place for the frail and timid people who easily get bruised. I was in the subway one day, for example, when the train arrived at my destination, 23rd Street. Instead of battling to get out of the door like everybody else, in the manner of a true English gentleman, I let them all go first and then attempted to go out. Just at that moment however, the electric doors closed in my face and the train was already on its way to another part of the city. The spark of chivalry within me was extinguished forever. Nobody knew how to get back to 23rd Street. Nobody in New York knows how to get anywhere. Some of the people who were asked embarked on a long rambling explanation and then admitted they did not know. Others said that where I was might not the best place to start from. One lady seemed to have a perfect knowledge of the shortest route back, but unfortunately spoke with such a marked Brooklyn accent that it was impossible to understand a word she said.

Many New Yorkers were grossly overfed and again, that is perhaps one of the overriding impressions we have of America even today. For a fortnight every meal I had was taken in a different restaurant, and I saw a great number of excessively corpulent and rotund gentlemen with fat cheeks like the gills of a turkey cock, which wobbled and shook as they ate. It seemed that some were so satiated that they had stomach to do no more than mess their food about with a fork. The food, of course, was magnificent. The stupendous variety of meals can be gauged from the fact that in one restaurant I was offered fourteen different kinds of potatoes. They were Allumette, Saute, Lyonnaise, Saratoga, Julienne, Hashed Brown, Au Gratin, Hashed Cream, Cottage Fried, Sweet, Candied, Florida, Imperial, and just fried!

When I had dined in London the previous August with some American social workers, who had just arrived in England, they told me of their astonishment upon seeing the drab and dirty buildings of London. It seemed strange at the time but I could understand now what they meant, for New York seemed like one of the cleanest cities in the world. Most of the sky scrapers were of recent construction and presented a dazzlingly clean, cream appearance in the sunlight. But they would not remain like this for very long unless great care was taken to keep smoke and dirt out of the city. For example, I was amazed to learn that no coal burning locomotives were allowed to come within twenty minutes distance of the railway terminus. Some miles outside the engines were taken off and the train was pulled into the station by electricity – and that was one of the most sensible things I ever heard. Neither did there seem to be factories which belched forth volumes of smoke. From seventy floors up in the Rockefeller Plaza not a single chimney stack could be seen across the diversified panorama of the city. Therefore, compared with most British centres of population, New York scintillated like a bride upon her wedding day. The City Council took pride in its insistence upon clean lines both in the streets and in other public places. All restaurants were frequently inspected, and scrupulous in their attempts to remain in the good books of the authorities.

To walk down the amazing Broadway at midnight was the sensation of a lifetime. Perhaps it may be best described as a highly concentrated mass of multi-coloured neon lights. The effect would be bad enough if this dazzling bally-hoo had stayed still, but when half the night signs were on the go as moving pictures, the effect was a deafening visual screech. Thousands of elaborate and vivid neons vied with each other in their power to catch the eye and baffle the imagination, and at night the whole of Times Square was turned into a giant kaleidoscope of continuously changing and dazzling colour. London at its brightest was in perpetual blackout compared with this.

Appropriately enough Broadway was the heart of New York's theatre land. There were very few ordinary shops in this part of the city and the whole area was a thickly assembled conglomeration of theatres, cinemas, restaurants, nightclubs, drugstores, hotels and amusement arcades, many of which places stayed open all night. Cabs came and went in a continuous stream. The music of a dozen orchestras rose upon the midnight air above the noise of traffic and the babble of crowds. Unearthly-looking people emerged from shining limousines onto the pavement, for some theatre performance. Women so glorious that they almost invited translation into some more ethereal world – and older ones too, who had succeeded in disguising the ravages of time with such barbarity that one wondered whether these creatures can belong to the human race at all. They were the opulent who, with their men-folk, herded themselves together in exotic apartments on Park Avenue, Fifth Avenue and Central Park. Yet were no more typical of ordinary American life than the Governor of the Bank of England was a typical Englishman.

Naturally, there was another side of life to be seen in New York away from all the glitz and glamour, and you didn't need to walk far to find it. Turn east from Fifth Avenue at its richest, and you would see blocks where the struggle for existence was manifest in tousled eating places and drab saloons, or the shops where women bought dresses off the massed hangers and came out wearing them; or regions where saloon windows announced, 'We buy pawn tickets' and signs outside barber shops which said, 'Black eyes made natural'.

When I was in New York, the truckers strike was on. It seemed to make no difference to the general run of life, but in accompaniment with it there was all kinds of little strikes going forward. Any single store could stage one of its own. A small hairdressers' establishment in a side street was picketed by its aggrieved employees. A department store on 23rd Street was in the throes of one. Round and round in a flattened circle on the pavement tramped the pickets before the shop entrance chanting briskly:

Wages are low and prices are high
So stay outside and don't you buy.

Three policemen with their backs to the shop window were swinging their clubs gently to the song.

There is much else that could be said about New York. The

skyscrapers alone deserve a volume to themselves, for this tremendous skyward thrusting mass of buildings that occupies the island of Manhattan is the greatest unplanned aggregation of architecture in the world. Awe-struck visitors regard the angular outlines of the city as one of the great sights of the modern world. True enough New York's impressive skyline is an architectural symbol of the deep-rooted American philosophy of rugged individualism. Its skyscrapers and mammoth slab-like surfaces jostle each other in a tense and dramatic battle that expresses as nothing else does the vital, competitive rush and struggle of American life.

Before leaving for Hartford, Connecticut, where I was to study, I made a short trip down into New Jersey, and with several of my colleagues, was entertained to dinner by the Committee for War Victims and Reconstruction at the New York Arts Club, with a visit to the Majestic Theater to see *Carousel*. I'd intended to spend a few days in Washington but at the last moment decided to leave it until the spring.

On Saturday 14 September, on my arrival in Hartford, the state capital of Connecticut, I was met by Dr English whose acquaintance I had previously made during his countrywide tour of England the preceding November. During the next three days I attended lectures by Dr HE Kirk, pastor for forty-five years of Franklin Street Presbyterian Church in Baltimore, and one of the outstanding theologians of America. He ploughed up our minds pretty thoroughly and sowed some choice seeds. It appears that Dr English's hobby during these days was introducing me to as many people as he could round up, and in the famous words of FC Knowles, "I shook hands so many times that the blood ran out from the tips of my fingers!"

The following Sunday I went with Dr English to a small country church about twenty-five miles away. Here he was booked to preach, but suggested to me that I should deliver the sermon while he conducted the rest of the service. This I did, and it produced something of a sensation; not because it was a good sermon but it must have been the first time these Yankee farmers had ever seen or heard such a foreign phenomenon. Not one of the locals took his eyes off me from beginning to end. They all sat on the edges of their seats and riveted their attention upon me as though I were a kind of trapeze act. Then afterwards one woman committed the indiscretion of saying to Dr English what an excellent idea it was that Mr Grant preached instead of him!

Hartford was an exceptionally pleasant place, reminding me of Leamington Spa. Natural parks and gardens extended over large areas within the city boundary. Vast numbers of trees lined the roads and grew in the gardens of the houses so that the whole place seemed to be cut clean out of the virgin forest. In the autumn, owing to the predominance of maple, the landscape was ablaze with the most gorgeous colours, the leaves turning from green to yellow, gold, red, purple and brown. I spent a weekend in the Berkshire Hills just at the right time, and drove through the most exquisite countryside across hills of rolling fire.

The Hartford Seminary Foundation was one of the foremost theological schools in the USA. It comprised three separate institutions – the Theological Seminary, the Kennedy School of Missions and the School of Religious Education. They worked independently in academic matters, each with its own Dean, but in everything else the three schools were as one and the students lived in halls of residence and joined together for their social and academic life.

The Seminary buildings stood on about thirty acres of ground, half of which was forest and of course completely open to the road. The profusion of the trees provided shelter for hundreds of squirrels which ran quite tamely on the ground and even got inside buildings.

There were about 200 students including about fifty single women, ten bachelors and about forty-five married couples. Male students were allowed to marry during their three year course of study and many took advantage of this doubtful privilege. Married quarters were provided and there were facilities for children. This did not mean that these people were any older than British students, but then, the USA was a country of early marriages. For example, there was a first year student of about twenty-eight who during his period of study was trying to support a wife and five children. Some of the wives attended lectures with their husbands, and there was a nursery school on the campus to which mothers took their children before they attended classes.

This was solely a post-graduate 'University of Religion', and all the inmates had degrees of some kind. It was interdenominational and international, but although some fifteen different nationalities were represented, I was the only Englishman. We took turns in returning thanks before meals and often it was done in such languages as French, Dutch, Hindi, Syrian, Norwegian, etc. On one occasion it was actually done in English – by me!

The night of the official opening of the academic year was one of solemn pomp and ceremony – rather like something out of the Arabian Nights. We were all standing assembled for the academic staff to enter in dignified procession. There was silence, and the tension was heightened because the cavalcade did not make its appearance until five minutes after the appointed time. An almost audible relief rippled through the assembled company when the pageant of professors rustled through the doorway. It was preceded by a strangely costumed official called the Marshall. I call him the mace-bearer because with great decorum he carried a thick metal rod greatly resembling a burglar's jemmy, which glistened all over with jewels. Because the procession moved so slowly I liked to think that the thing was a mine detector in disguise in case the students had planted mines below the floor boards in order to blow up the whole faculty before the theological slavery could be started. I could appreciate the gowns and hoods, of course, but some of these people wore golden crusted mortarboards with gold tassels. The climax of the whole ceremony came when the President said in an awesome voice, "I declare the academic year now open." It was a job to stop myself from laughing out loud!

There was nothing in this seminary resembling a juniority policy and seniority carried with it no special privileges. There was no such thing as 'high-table' and members of the faculty sat for their meals anywhere among the students. This caused no embarrassment and we enjoyed the table fellowship of the professors. Nearly all the kitchen and dining room work was done by the students, some of whom found this necessary in order to remain financially solvent.

The equivalent of our 'houses' was the Student Association – a very loosely knit organisation which held its meetings once a quarter. Subordinate to this were the local associations of the various halls of residence on the campus.

Perhaps this might be the right place to say a word about food again. Although the meals provided were not up to the standard of those we had in the restaurants, they compared very favourably with the heavy and sombre diet of Manchester. Typically we had:

Breakfast: fruit juice, cereal, buckwheat cakes, coffee.
Lunch: tomato juice, oysters in soup, lemon pie, milk.
Dinner: apple juice, meat hash with maize salad, ice cream, coffee.

All meals were formal, which meant that we could not come and go as we liked. Classes began at 8am and went through until 5pm. When I first arrived I noticed with astonishment that people did not even think of drinking mid-morning or mid-afternoon tea or coffee. I was compelled very often during the morning and again at night to go up to the drug store at the end of the road for a hot dog or a bacon sandwich.

The official social life on the campus was small but sometimes we were treated to an evening of American folk dancing in the social room of the women's hall, which was a rather less pleasant experience than it sounds.

61

Chapter Five

America, Coast to Coast

I was in Hartford, Connecticut, from September 1946 to June 1947, and there I received the degree of Bachelor of Divinity. The Hartford Seminary Foundation maintained a high academic standard, and the students there had a perpetual struggle to meet a virtually unending series of deadlines on papers, exams, books and other assignments. And in connection with this, the authorities had a most inconvenient system whereby papers remaining unfinished at the deadline received a lower grade. More than once I heard of a pyjama-clad professor shivering upon his snow-covered doorstep after having been awakened to receive the work of students, who had toiled at breakneck speed to make the midnight deadline.

It was a pleasure to work for some professors, and an inspiration to sit day by day at their feet. Most of them were well-known and eminent in scholarship. There was Matthew Spinka, for example, professor of Church History, a master of thirteen languages, and an authority on Russian Communism, author of books and graduate of many universities; there was Karl Lowith, professor of the Philosophy of Religion. He and his family were driven successively from Germany, Italy and Japan by the respective governments of those countries, and had now found a more congenial habitat in the 'land of the free'.

But there were one or two – as in every place of learning – who were fiascos. Perhaps the only really tragic figure was the lecturer on Principles of Preaching, whose twitterings had to be listened to every afternoon at the soporific hour of 2pm. We soon came to call it the 'Principles of Sleeping', for the only way we could prop open our eyelids was by turning round to see how the men behind were doing it.

The lecturer himself – a Christian gentleman if there ever was one – was, as a lecturer, surely unbeatably the world's worst. For one hour there droned across the room a continuous lullaby of ungrammatical and almost meaningless drivel, which never once had any apparent connection with the principles of preaching, and to which no one attempted to listen. We were there, our presence was recorded, and the hour was a godsend for letter writing and other urgent work. Amusingly enough, our lecturer was the supreme example of every bad practice in preaching, and if ever any of us became good preachers, it would be because we strove mightily not to be like him.

Incidentally, this man refused to let me take a written exam on account of my bad writing, so I sat in his office for two and a half hours and was plied with such absurd questions as, "Who started the Crusades?" But good or bad, every professor required a maximum output of the students' best.

Work was our meat and drink, but it did not prove to be a body-building substitute for the rather poor meals served in the Seminary dining hall. Only once during the whole year was the breakfast menu of coffee, rolls, or the dreaded hot-cakes broken in favour of anything else. On one occasion a student gave a grace something like this: "O Lord, we pray that Thou wilt give us the strength to eat this food, and comfort us afterward, Amen." When my turn came, I was sorely tempted to say, quite simply, "O Lord, lay not this sin to their charge."

Yet, all in all, life at Hartford was rich and exciting. The spirit of fellowship in the student body and faculty provided a memorable context within which the toil and leisure of the days progressed. Weekend speaking trips brought ever-new glimpses of the exquisitely wooded New England countryside, and gave extensive opportunity to learn of the American people in their homes. Without exception they were gracious and kind, curious to hear about conditions in England,

and fiercely proud of even the remotest English ancestry.

As my financial solvency was partly dependent upon such trips, I was always bound to have a keen, though concealed, interest in the fee for my talk or sermon. Sometimes I was allowed to depart with neither fee nor expenses, but there were several places which paid me at the rate of a dollar a minute – this was generosity indeed. But, not to be out-done, I felt it only charitable sometimes, to throw in a couple of extra minutes without charge.

Except in the case of preaching engagements, most groups wanted to hear about some aspect of British life. Kiwanis and Rotary clubs were anxious to know what I thought of the Labour government and how socialism was working out. Ministers' fraternals were treated to a discourse on 'the theological scene in England today'; cosmopolitan clubs were interested in British foreign policy – particularly in relation to India and Palestine. Church groups were eager to be told about the churches in Britain, and nearly everybody found something worthwhile listening to in talks on England during the war, and British customs and traditions.

The 1,000 photographs of Britain I brought over came in useful several times, as for example, when I gave a lecture in the town hall in Coventry on 'Coventry, before and after the Blitz'. Incidentally, when the lecture was over, the first question to be asked was, "What are the hair-cutting methods now in use in England?" One had to be prepared for anything, and I explained that it was all done with scissors.

Much more could be said about the colourful cosmopolitan student life on the campus with its different nationalities. In the autumn, the Great International Festival presented the Arabs, Czechs, Koreans, Dutch, Chinese, Indians, Norwegians, Syrians, English and others, in the pomp and pageantry of their respective countries.

I was particularly friendly with the Norwegian families who were on furlough from their missionary work in North Africa. The young children, for whom I played Santa Claus at Christmas time, had some strange language difficulties. They were desperately struggling with the complexities of three – Norwegian, their native tongue; French, spoken in Algeria; and English, which is the language purported to be used in this country.

A Czech student, Zdenek Bednar, was also striving to learn the lingo. When coming to this country after six weeks instruction, he spoke remarkably well, yet it was inevitable that there should be some howlers. For example; upon being invited by a student's mother to spend Christmas at their home, he expressed great delight, and went around asking everybody's advice about what present he could buy, "in revenge for the invitation".

A Dutch student – with whom I maintained a friendship throughout the year to everyone's horror – had to be seen to be believed. The daughter of a famous European theologian, she was a charming rebel against authority. On a campus where women smokers and flamboyant dresses were highly disapproved, Anna smoked like a chimney and sported a thick, shapeless coat with wide stripes of red, green and white. To pay for room, board, and tuition, she was compelled to work long hours in the student dining room, at fifty cents an hour. Once she said to me half in jest, "I would do a murder for $100." But in spite of such wild pronouncements, I was never ill at ease. Always short of money, she found it highly advantageous to make sure I invited her to the local drug store every evening at 10pm, after the library closed. Sitting on stools at the counter, we would astonish everybody by chanting French and English poetry in unison.

Less sensational, but more profitable ventures were those in which Anna and I made joint public appearances to speak about our respective countries. Her English, French and German were excellent, though spoken with a marked Dutch accent, and her fiery dramatic styles always had people sitting on the edges of their seats. Often we were asked to tell of our war experiences. The stories of my escapes in the big blitzes would always be overshadowed by her breath-taking narrative of dangerous exploits in the Dutch underground movement.

Our close association was resented by those who considered it wrong for an engaged girl to have male friends, and the backbiting was especially vengeful among those who wanted desperately to become engaged, but who had given up hope of ever being so. Anna's fiancé was studying Chinese at Harvard, and came down every three weeks, and he and I came to be real friends. To emphasise the solidarity of our relationship, we would sit on either side of Anna at mealtimes in the dining hall. Actually, Anna's fiancé was grateful for the close friendship which she and I had formed, for it served to protect her from the amorous advances of those who respected her betrothal less than I.

The days at Hartford raced away with inconsiderate speed. Final examinations were soon upon us, and happy was that morning in May 1947 when we received our bachelor's 'ticket' and the approbation of the cheering multitude.

On 7 June that year I started upon a three month speaking tour which lasted for 10,000 miles through twenty-six states and part of Canada. The first trip outside New England was 1,300 miles down into Florida. At the office of my committee in New York, the secretary tried to make Pullman reservations by telephone. Her conversation with the ticket office girl at the other end went something like this:

Sec: I want to make a reservation on the 11.30 'Silver Meteor' for Florida on Sunday.
Girl: Sorry, not a thing left.
Sec: Are you sure there's not even one?
Girl: Positively nothing.
Sec: Well, this is for the Reverend CH Grant.
Girl: Did you say the Reverend?
Sec: Yes.
Girl: (Hastily) Wait a minute, I'll see what we have!

The next day I boarded the luxurious, chromium plated 'Silver Meteor' for that delectable peninsula. My ticket, which contained detachable sections for every railroad I was to travel on during the journey, was nearly eighteen inches long, and cost $80. It would have been nearly twice as much except for the fact that in the USA, ministers of all denominations were entitled to travel for half the fare on some railroads – a very useful concession.

The train soon passed through Philadelphia – 'the city of brotherly love' – and Baltimore, both of which were remarkable only for their dinginess and tiny red-brick houses. But Washington was different. The capital appeared to be a spacious noble city. In the gathering dusk, the massive white pillared dome of the Capitol rose majestically above the skyline, and on the way south the 560 foot needle of the Washington Monument drew the admiring gaze of all on the train.

As darkness fell, we entered the state of Virginia and crossed the Mason-Dixon Line, which technically separates the northern USA from the southern USA, with its different customs, traditions and laws.

Then, the embers of that Civil War still smouldered with uncomfortable heat in national affairs. The focal disagreement was over the status of the black American and the right of each state to govern its own internal affairs without regard to the authority of the federal government. The federal government gave black Americans the rights and privileges of first class citizens, but the southern states enacted counter-legislation hostile to him, and southern practice treated him as if he were no citizen at all.

The result of all was that below the Mason-Dixon Line the black American was virtually without human rights, and completely at the mercy of the white man. It was not unheard of that if a black man failed to say "Sir" when speaking to a white man, he was beaten up; or if he failed to step off into the gutter when a white man passed at a place on the pavement too narrow for two, he was deliberately knocked down.

In the north, of course, and particularly among enlightened people, there was great dissatisfaction with this situation. Matters were brought to something of a climax in July 1948 when, with President Truman's insistence upon the inclusion of a Civil Rights plant in the

Democratic campaign platform, a large section of Southern Democrats broke away, calling themselves the Dixiecrats. They nominated their own candidate for president – Strom Thurmond, Governor of Georgia. This man had a large following in Dixie, and was supported by the powerful black-hating, secret society, the Ku Klux Klan. "If Truman tries to force civil rights on the south," they warned, "blood will flow in the streets."

The first example I witnessed of how civil rights were denied to black people came immediately as our train passed over the Mason-Dixon Line. I was in the dining car at the time and two black men, who were eating with the rest of us when the train entered Virginia, were asked by the steward to take themselves to the partitioned off section of the dining car marked 'colored'. This was 'lawfully' necessary because, in the southern states, black people were forbidden to associate with whites. They were forbidden to eat in the same restaurants, forbidden to sit with white people in cinemas, and forbidden to ride in the same section of a public vehicle with white people; hence the dining car incident. In the same way, it was against the law for people of the two races to join together in a church for public worship. Professor G Buell Gallagher, with whom I worked for a year in California, was once fined over $300 in Alabama for sitting – just sitting – in a black restaurant. Several times his life was threatened because he entertained black people at his home. At the time he was president of Talladega College, a Congregational institution for blacks in the state of Alabama.

The Pullman car had one of the most ingeniously compact sleeping arrangements ever invented. The car was divided into twenty sections, with two passengers to a section sitting opposite each other. At night time, the two seats combined to make a lower berth, while a section of the wide coach above the passenger's head was pulled down by the porter to form an upper berth. Both of these berths were as large as full-sized single beds and a small stepladder gave access to the upper. Complete privacy was assured on three sides by the sectional limits, and on the corridor side, by thick green curtains. It gave one a magnificent sense of well-being to slip into cool, clean sheets as the train rumbled on through the night. It was also quite exciting to have one's first peep through a window in the morning to see what kind of country the train had reached after eleven or twelve hours of darkness and five or six hundred miles of progress.

In contrast to the rolling hills of Virginia, the Georgian country was flat and well wooded. Dotted about here and there were the pitiful wooden shacks of share-croppers – the forgotten men of the south – black and white. It was a rather sorry landscape.

The train stopped at Savannah, Georgia and, after having come nearly 1,000 miles from New York, I thought it would be interesting to go outside and test the temperature. The air was furnace-like, and the breeze a sirocco, for already the thermometer had reached ninety-two degrees Fahrenheit in the shade.

In a few hours we were well down into Florida. The kind of country seen from the window was – for the first 200 miles – thinly populated, flat derelict woodland, broken here and there by great empty patches of swamp. The interminable mass of green and brown was now and again relieved, startlingly, by the appearance of enormous white egrets.

It would have been surprising if my arrival in Florida had not been marked by brilliant sunshine, yet the very next day a total of twelve inches of rain fell in only nine hours. It was a truly Manchurian effort; in between torrential showers the sun would come out, and in the hot, still air masses of steam would rise from the sodden yellow soil and dripping trees. It was a kind of vast natural Turkish bath.

But this is getting ahead. When the train arrived at the little orange grove town of Avon Park I was whisked away by car to an outlying country mansion. It was a huge log-built edifice overlooking a tropical palm-fringed lake, and accommodating one hundred people. The place was owned by the Congregational churches of Florida, and used for conferences, vacations and so on. That evening about 100 teenagers, bursting with energy and good humour, had just settled in to begin their annual week of what is called 'Conference'. Actually, 'Conference' was a combination of carefree holidaying and serious study.

Immediately after lunch there would be a rest hour, then various occupational activities such as handicrafts, singing, painting, etc. After one hour of this, the highly anticipated recreational period would begin and continue until supper-time. Basketball, baseball and swimming were all enjoyed, but swimming was the favourite. Indeed, to disport oneself in that delectable lake was almost an excursion into *Alice in Wonderland*. On every little beach the luxuriant fronded date-palms swept down upon the surface of the water. To step in for the first time was a delight – there was no shivering, miserable moment of hesitation upon the bank, for the water was temptingly lukewarm, and gave one the feeling, as it closed upon the body, that a long-lost natural habitat had at last been rediscovered. And certainly, if one may judge by the prowess and colour of those gliding teenagers, they had spent more of their lives in the water than out.

But that was not all. The floor of the lake was of pure white sand, and the water so crystal-clear that, at twenty foot deep, patches of the dazzling whiteness shone in undiminished radiance through the tangled emerald green of the water plants. Moreover, shoals of brightly coloured tropical fish swam near the surface, their yellow blue and red scales reflecting brilliantly in the sunlight. No wonder there was a general reluctance to get dressed, even for supper. After this evening meal a vesper hour of hymns, prayers, and a short homily by the conference chaplain, was held, and then there would be two or three hours of games, movies, and dancing.

It was during these times that I gradually came to learn, and then dislike – eventually hate folk-dancing. It was probably because I had no natural aptitude for such complex bodily contortions. I could never remember the special vocabulary used to describe the names of the movements, nor, could I ever learn the order in which they came.

And of course, as far as serious-minded people are concerned, if a folk-dance is to be successful everybody must know how, and when, and what to do. Now, I never had the slightest ability in such precise cavorting. It has the dull, inhuman perfection of machinery. The only interest I could ever master in the dance was when everything went wrong, and on those wretched occasions when I took part nothing ever went right. My attempts to keep up with the music and follow the actions of the other dancers were pitiful to behold, and on those rare occasions when I did not completely wreck the whole proceedings, to receive the congratulations of the others made me feel no better. Once, in a particularly energetic caper, when great lines of people were twisting and charging about at speed, I made a fatal wrong turn into such a line, and it bore down upon me with such irresistible power and rapidity that every one of its members piled up on top of me in a sprawling heap. Besides coming near to asphyxiation by the weight of bodies, I was almost shrivelled to a crisp by the multitudinous oaths heaped upon me by my religious colleagues of the dance. Needless to say, I have done no folk-dancing since!

The time passed pleasantly enough in Florida, except that every day I had to speak for two hours on the general subject of 'the post-war european scene', which was something of a strain. But I managed to get through it, and as I journeyed north again I was given a cheery send-off by those incredulous youngsters who had learned where the British Isles are, that England is not perpetually blanketed in fog, and that some people in Europe do not have enough to eat. The steaming orange groves, the unearthly beautiful lake, and the six inch multicoloured butterflies weaving their fitful course among the scarlet hibiscus – all this had to be left behind.

Once more I was in New York, and then, after a few days at a private school deep in the undulating hills of southern Connecticut, went up to another conference in New Hampshire. This was by way of Rhode Island and Boston.

Lake Winnepesaukee, at the foot of the White Mountains, was

the largest of several thousand lakes in New Hampshire. The whole surrounding country and numerous islands which break up the expanse of water was densely forested. From the weirs on the lake shore it took two and a half hours to reach Guernsey Island, while sitting on top of a toy-like US mail steamer. Here, living conditions were very different from those of Wooster School in Connecticut, which was the last place I had been, and where I had occupied a master's private suite. But on Guernsey Island only the roughest and barest camp facilities prevailed. In this practically virgin country, sleeping at night in crude wooden shacks, without windows or screens, and even without adequate sanitary arrangements, I came nearer to feeling like a Pilgrim Father than ever before, or since.

There was one impressive thing about this five-day visit to Lake Winnepesaukee, and that was the open-air candlelight service on the last night. This ceremony was a part of the routine of nearly every conference, but here it was strangely inspiring. When darkness fell everyone gathered on the lake shore. Candles were passed out to the 150 persons present, and were lit by the medium of a single master-flame. Then in the absolute silence of night we wended our way single file through the trees, each carrying his candle. At a certain signal everyone began to sing the rousing hymn *Follow the Gleam*. Very soon the forest was filled with twinkling lights and those at the end of the line would hear the distant voices of the first ones, now high on the hill, yet the direct light of their candles would be hidden by the intervening trees. At last, when a clearing in the woods had been reached, everyone stood in a circle while the chaplain spoke a prayer.

From Winnepesaukee it was only a few hours journey down to Cape Cod, Massachusetts. Here again the lakeside setting was superbly beautiful, and it was good to sleep out in the open under the stars. This could not be done without mosquito nets, of course. (Up in New Hampshire I had been cut nearly to pieces by the insects.) The four-day visit to Cape Cod afforded the opportunity for a unique experience – that of seeing the actual (supposed) place where the

Pilgrim Fathers landed in 1620. The town of Plymouth is a gracious, tradition-laden village which the guide books would call 'quaint'. The Plymouth Rock itself, however, is something of a farce. A grey, oval shaped piece of stone, weighing about half a ton, and with the year 1620 carved on its smooth face, rested on the shore and was protected from souvenir hunters by an elaborate, house-sized covering, complete with an iron grill and fake Doric columns. We were told this was the little piece of America upon which founders of these United States first set foot as they stepped off the Mayflower. Tourists gazed upon it with evident fascination, but whether, after all these centuries, its authenticity could be guaranteed seemed more than doubtful. The question may be asked whether the Pilgrim Fathers could themselves remember, after a couple of weeks, the exact rock upon which they landed. They had other things to think about.

So the miles, the conferences, the speeches and the talks piled up in the ensuing weeks. Possibly the most elaborate and successful conference of all the fifteen I attended was that at Blair Academy in New Jersey. Here were over 300 young people from the state of New York, and a faculty of forty, including experts on Palestine, India and physical education. The first two gave me a severe dressing-down, in the evils of British policy in those countries, in a manner which suggested that they thought I was solely responsible. The third might have been equally reprimanding had he known that I could not touch my toes! There was also an expert newspaper-printing person and hand, who every day, with the help of aides, produced a remarkably good sheet providing first hand accounts of conference news and views.

The great journey of nearly 3,000 miles to the Pacific coast, where I was to remain for a year, began from Springfield, Massachusetts.

Only an hour from Buffalo is the city of Niagara Falls, renowned for Shredded Wheat and of course the falls. It is difficult to know if the town is one place or two, for the US Canadian frontier cuts the city in half.

Niagara was hardly distinguishable from thousands of other small American towns and, as one walked along Main Street, it was almost impossible to believe that around the corner, just a couple of hundred yards further on, there suddenly opened up that breathless spectacle which people came from every corner of the globe to see.

The pen is powerless, and the camera quite inadequate to convey an impression of what these thunderous cascades are like. Imagine a mighty river plunging over a precipice 2,000 foot wide and 160 foot deep, and so dazzling white as the sun shines upon it that it almost blinds your eyes. As the glittering mass tumbles headlong, and strikes the bottom, imagine a roar so great that it sounds like peeling thunder and makes the human voice inaudible. Imagine blinding clouds of spray rising hundreds of feet from the seething cauldron at the base of the fall, blocking out the view, and drenching un-waterproofed spectators to the skin. Imagine all this, and you will have but a remote idea of what an experience it is to see, hear, and feel a million and a half gallons of water a second go over the top. I stood for over a half-an-hour, fascinated and entranced – so near to the water I could almost touch it.

After this, I went across the Rainbow Bridge (it marks the USA Canadian frontier) connecting the two precipices over the river just below the falls. In order to get a good view of the American Falls it is necessary to go to the Canadian side – and vice versa.

I was much surprised when, as a British subject, I was refused admission to a territory of the then British Empire. The explanation was that if I were admitted to Canada I should lose my status as a British non-quota immigrant to America, and would be refused entry into the USA again when I returned after only half an hour. This was preposterous, but nothing could be done about it, so I had to go back to the American side of the bridge. But the immigration inspector there was not convinced that I had not set foot upon Canadian soil, and would not let me through. This was a dilemma indeed, and I had momentary visions of myself taking up residence on the bridge for the rest of my life. The only way I got back was by asking the inspector to telephone the Canadian authorities for confirmation of my story.

The same difficulty, but in a much worse form, was encountered when I tried to travel to Detroit from Niagara across Ontario. All USA trains were sealed while crossing this section of Canada, so that for me it would not be considered a voluntary departure from the country. But the difficulty came when a lack of suitable rail connections compelled me to take a bus to Welland, fifteen miles inside Canada to join the train there. When the frontier was reached the Canadian inspectors refused to let me proceed – no doubt for my own good – and turned me back in view of the fact that a few steps from the bus to the train would constitute a voluntary transference to alien soil. There was no alternative but to go back to Niagara and Buffalo, and there wait for five hours for a through train to Detroit. When at last, in the early hours of the morning, I did arrive at the world's greatest motor manufacturing centre I had had no sleep for two nights. The next day I had to preach to 2,000 people at the great Bushnell Congregational Church.

The church was in every way different from the rest of Detroit. A large place, in the old New England portico style, its most striking feature was that everything inside was painted pure white. The only exceptions were the royal blue carpet in the aisles and the blue velvet on the high-backed chairs on the rostrum. The effect of having only two colours in the building was indescribably beautiful. The church was thriving and well-to-do, with 1,000 pupils in the Sunday school and 2,000 in the congregation. The offering at a single service was usually between $2,000 and $2,500 (£500–600), and on the Monday morning at eleven o'clock was called for by an armoured car. I watched this happen and wondered where else in the world there could be seen the phenomenon of an armed guard complete with holster, revolver, ammunition belt, checking over the Sunday collection.

Then it was on to the Midwest, by and large an uninteresting area. Twelve hundred miles from the nearest sea, it is not surprising that in this heart of the USA I should find people more ignorant of world affairs than those nearer the three coasts – even some who did not know where the British Isles are. They were sceptical of the British Labour government and had little interest, apparently, in the fate of other countries beyond the conviction that the spread of Communism must be checked.

One of the satisfying results of talking to Rotary clubs, and others in the face of this kind of indoctrination, was that hard-boiled isolationists, business men and farmers sometimes asked me, after the meeting, what they could do to help Europeans in their struggle for life and rehabilitation. At least one thing they did – and for the first time in their lives – was to send twenty or thirty dollars of food across the sea.

The long trek across the seemingly interminable, deadly, flat, plain lands of Missouri and Kansas was, to put it mildly, dull.

Yet it was something of a thrill to make my way gradually into the Wild West. One morning I arrived at the colourful and romantic Rocky Mountain town of Denver, gateway to some of the most magnificent mountain scenery anywhere on the continent, as well as the fabulous old-time gold and silver mines. Here, for the first time on the way west, one saw cowboy equipment for sale in all the clothing stores – high-heeled, gaily decorated leather boots with spurs, and the broad brimmed, high peaked stetsons.

The tradition of largeness which is associated with the West and all its works was symbolized for me that morning when, in the station restaurant, I saw a woman eating a slice of watermelon; or rather, I presumed that there must have been someone behind the gigantic dripping crescent standing at one of the tables. I could not think it was unattended, and I was right, for when I went round to the other side of the two-foot-high piece of fruit, a lady was digging pieces out of it with her spoon. I had indeed arrived in the fabulous West.

One of the most typically Western places in Colorado was Walsenburg, a lonely, remote little town 170 miles south of Denver and only forty miles from the border of New Mexico. Even in those unenlightened days, Walsenburg was, shall we say, a care-free town. Before I went to bed on the first night, I was told that to put a revolver under my pillow would be a wise precaution, and that the procedure would be to shoot first, and ask questions later. My twenty-two and a half stone host – the Congregational minister – always had a .45 automatic in constant readiness. This rip-roaring town possessed fifteen grocery stores and fifty-seven public houses.

As can be imagined, it was something of an occasion for an Englishman to come into town. My forthcoming visit had been hailed for several days in the local press (which had the flamboyant name of *World Independent*). When at last I did show up, a headline proclaimed 'CH Grant Arrives in City Today'. Then there was a list, with time and places, of all I intended to do, and the meetings I was scheduled to address. One day some old ladies gave a dinner in my honour. This was reported together with the names of all present. Before I left, the *World Independent* really outdid itself and prevailed upon me for an official interview. It appeared the following day together with an appropriate headline and was given a full three-quarters of a page. An Englishman in Colorado must have been a rare bird indeed, as the following incident will testify. About fifty miles north of Walsenburg is the town of Pueblo with 50,000 people. In the main street I stopped at a publicity place to get a map of the Colorado Valley. The girl asked me to sign the visitors book, and I did. No further words passed between us. Next day in the *Pueblo Chieftain* was a full account of the proceeding under the headline, 'Tourist from England Visits Information Hut'.

I did not leave this fascinating area without making an excursion up into the Rockies. They were much like the Swiss Alps in their rugged grandeur and the marvellous panorama they provided for the climber. There was a real difference, however, and that is that owing to their southern latitude the Colorado Rockies have a very high timberline, and below Denver are not perpetually snow-capped. I ascended over

11,000 feet and at that height the slopes were still forested.

A word may be said here about automobile riding in these regions. Cars which travel at great heights over the mountain passes are often fitted with altimeters, and sometimes on the highest roads boiling radiators will be only lukewarm. Of course, most of the passes which cross the Rockies, at the lofty elevation of ten to twelve thousand feet, were blocked by impenetrable snow for more than seven months of the year. Yet in summer, the heat would be so intense that motor car travel became almost impossible to bear unless an air-cooler is used. A familiar sight on cars that journey across the scorching 1,000 mile wide desert land of the south-west was that of water-bags hanging on the outside. In view of the fact that one could drive for 200 miles without seeing a single habitation or sign of water, it was of the utmost importance to carry an extra supply. On the ruler-straight lovely roads of the West there was little hardship in driving 600 miles a day. Distance meant nothing, and I myself had been driven sixty miles by people with whom I was staying, merely to go to a restaurant for dinner. A common sight all over the USA was the 'motel' which, as its name suggests, was an unpretentious hotel for motorists and which promised sleeping accommodation only. In this country gasoline was twenty-five cents a gallon but, as most of the cars were of 100 horse power, a gallon lasts only a few miles.

Life was made easier for the motorist in every possible way. One of the chief features of towns everywhere was the 'drive-in' – a circular shaped eating place up to the front of which a car may be driven, while waitresses (called 'car-hops') came out for the order and delivered the food to customers as they sat in their car. The trays of food were attached to a gadget on the inside of the car door. In some Californian towns, the car-hops were fitted with roller-skates, enabling them to get around faster.

Another invention for the benefit of the motorist was the outdoor cinema. These were being built all over the country. They were generally on the outskirts of a large town, and the auditorium resembled a huge parking lot. Cars drove in, an attendant cleaned the windscreen, and fixed a loudspeaker to the side of the car through which the sound came. The film could then be watched from the snug comfort of the car seat. This recreation was just as popular in the winter, for the cars were all equipped with heating apparatus. It may be understood that practically everyone in this country was dependent upon the motor car for travel. Many thousands of young people had never been on a train or even a bus. One lady heard me tell how few people in England were lucky enough to have a car. A bewildered look appeared on her face, and incredulously she asked, "Well, how do they get to work then?" It had not for a moment dawned on her that they might go by bus, train, or bicycle. Bicycles, incidentally, were almost unknown in this country, except among young people.

The next stage of the journey was through New Mexico and Arizona. It was not until the nineteenth century that white men first went into the great south-west, which, up until then was the home of a few Spaniards and Indians. As a result of the war with Mexico in 1848 both Arizona and New Mexico were ceded to the USA, and this ushered in one of the bloodiest periods in American frontier history. The Indian Wars, breeding a habit of dependence on force, and the heterogeneous elements of cattle thieves, Sonora cowboys, mine labourers, frontier jumpers, and adventurers, provided raw material for a good many Hollywood Western pictures.

The Indians were far more numerous in these two states than anywhere else, living on reservations hundreds of square miles in extent, and on land so poor that life could barely be sustained. Many of these people could not read or write and were able to speak only their native tribal tongue. I visited some of their primitive shacks in the Hopi country where the main source of income was derived from drying peaches. Social services were practically non-existent. On the Hopi reservation I went to, which contained several thousand Indians, there were no schools and not a single doctor. The US government seemed to have little interest in the fate of the poor, but friendly people, from whom this continent was originally seized.

The physical features of this vast south-western area were remarkable. Practically all of it was scrub and desert country on which rain rarely, if ever, fell. The sun shined at Phoenix, Arizona for eighty-eight per cent of the total possible time. Yet, desert or not, the panorama of scenery (it cannot in any sense of the word be called 'countryside') was always one to rivet attention. The colour green was almost never seen; the predominant shades were red, brown, yellow, and maroon. For hundreds of miles there was nothing but a constantly changing combination of these. Sometimes the train would pass through a desert mountain range, and the rugged terrain was often gashed by superb river canyons. Rivers, by the way, which never flowed unless high in the hills a flash-flood unleashed a raging tumult which pelted down as a vast scourge of God. It was rare indeed to see any signs of life, and rarer still to come upon a centre of population. But towns like Gallup, New Mexico presented an impressive sight. Indian squaws with colourful pleated ankle-length skirts, which almost looked like crinolines, carried their children sling-like upon their backs, while the men in cowboy pants and high black hats swaggered through the street.

When in Arizona, I was anxious to see the Grand Canyon – which is a stupendous feature, as Hollywood would say. And for once, Hollywood was not wrong. The Grand Canyon is a mighty gash in the earth, about 105 miles long, four to eighteen miles wide, and at some points 5,000 feet deep. No words can convey what it was like to stand on the rim and gaze into the depths of that mighty abyss. There, 5,000 feet down, the Colorado River lay like a tiny silver thread, seemingly motionless. Such a spectacle as this was almost overpowering in its impact upon the senses, and the only desire – even above that for food and rest – was to feast one's eyes interminably on this richly beautiful, yet terrifying sight.

In the gorge itself many traces of ancient life had been found – impressions of seaweed and other plants long extinct, tracks of animals and extinct forms of fish. Only a few years previously a hitherto unknown tribe of Indians was discovered living in a remote part of the canyon, and also a unique race of horse which, owing to centuries of inbreeding, are no larger than dogs.

On that hot August afternoon in 1947 I stood 7,000 feet above sea level on the canyon rim among the gnarled pinion trees and the cacti (some of which I dug up and sent to England in a box). The panorama was majestic and difficult to comprehend. The great temptation was to go down inside. This could be done by means of mules which carried one, in nerve-racking fashion, down a precipitous path about twelve inches wide. Sometimes the animals terrify their riders by stepping onto the edge of a 3,000 feet precipice in order to lean over for an especially succulent piece of grass. Accidents rarely happened, but when they do, they were always fatal.

In August and September I spent three weeks at a retreat in the San Bernardino mountains of Southern California. This area was semi-desert country, but irrigation had worked wonders in the production of oranges, dates, nuts, peaches etc. The retreat, Pilgrim Pines, was maintained by the Congregational Church of California and used for vacation conferences. I took part in five of these and, owing to the mile high elevation of this place, did not suffer from the heat which had previously caused me great discomfort. One Sunday, however, I had to go down in the valley to preach in the Congregational church at San Bernardino. There they had huge fans at work inside, but the shade temperature outside was 112 degrees Fahrenheit, and the fans were of little effect. Discomfort is not the word to use in connection with that incident. As I walked from the church, it seemed I could smell rubber burning from my soles, and indeed, I should have suffered severe burns had I laid my arm on the outside parts of my host's automobile.

Chapter Six

A not-so-Brief Encounter

Eventually I arrived on the Pacific coast of the USA and marvelled at its sheer beauty. Pages could be written about the 13,000 foot Sierra Nevada, the 5,000-year-old, 360 foot Redwood trees, and visits in this fascinating country to equally fascinating schools, clubs, and churches where poor congregations were excused on the grounds that the pheasant season had just started, or that the members had just gone on a bear hunt. No wonder I stayed a year, and amid this beauty and sunshine I was to experience one of the most life-changing years of my life, and quite unexpectedly too.

During my travels across the United States I had decided I should like to study for a Master's degree in Theology while in the country, and so, after some research, decided to apply to the Pacific School of Religion at the University of California, based at its sprawling Berkeley campus. This would take a year and I would live in the swashbuckling city of San Francisco, on the shores of its sunlit bay. Every night from my window I watched the sun sink with crimson glory through the Golden Gate into the Pacific Ocean. It must be said that it was a rather more impressive view than the one from the guest house in Margate.

The work was hard, and I had a long and involved thesis to write which I toiled and sweated over, night after night. This effort was made bearable by the companionship of my fellow students, who never regarded me as anything less than a curiosity from a far-flung island who had somehow landed up on Pacific shores and appeared to be settling in rather nicely.

One student in particular stood out. Every evening she walked across the campus to her lodgings, passing my window in the twilight. I became interested in this attractive young woman and decided to find out more about her. Perhaps my journalistic instincts hadn't been as neglected as I'd thought. One evening I saw her coming across the lawn carrying what appeared to be a heavy pile of books. This was my opportunity. I laid down my pen and scuttled out of my room, following in her wake. "Excuse me," I said, in my best native English accent, "those books look rather heavy. Would you like me to assist you with them?"

The young woman turned and smiled. "Thank you," she said, gratefully delivering the load into my arms. "You're most kind."

Well, the carrying of heavy books for Dolores Jeanette Mobley, aged twenty-nine, of Des Moines, Iowa, became a regular occurrence and during the walks we shared information about our lives. She had four brothers and came from a farming family. At the age of seventeen she'd left home for college in Sacramento, California. She went on to do a BA degree and eventually progressed to post graduate study, at the University of California, at Berkeley. During these years of study she had married and, just two years later, been tragically widowed.

It could have been a terrible mismatch. An American woman from a mid-west farming family and an Englishman from Bristol via Birmingham and Margate. What could we possibly have in common? She'd never been further east than Chicago and I was only here because I wasn't in Germany. At the time, Britain was almost indescribable to the average American; war-torn, poor, grey, austere, cold and damp. I was dazzled by America and Americans but even I knew that it was a kind of fantasy that I would one day have to leave behind in return for bleaker shores on the other side of the Atlantic.

But as they say, love conquers all and, by and by, we started to become very fond of one another. Not having much experience of this kind of thing, I mentally rehearsed ways I might convey my feelings to Dolores. One evening, as I carried her books as usual, I tentatively said to her, "You are getting on and I am getting on; don't you think it is time we settled down?" which both of us took as being a circumlocutory proposal of marriage. It was far from going down on one knee, but it worked.

Six months later we were joined in matrimony on 20 June 1948, at the Church for the Fellowship of All Peoples in San Francisco, where Dolores was part-time secretary. It was the first truly inter-racial, international church in the city, representing a wide range of nationalities. The minister was Dr Howard Thurman – a descendant of Negro slaves – whom *Life* magazine claimed to be one of the most powerful preachers in the USA.

The whole cost of the wedding was borne by the church apart from the licence fee, which was two dollars. When the Registrar handed it to me he said, "I think we shall have to put this up to $2.50 before people stop coming in for it!" It was an unusual wedding in many respects, one of them being that no member of either family was present. Mine was 5,000 miles away, hers 2,500, and they were in poor health.

In August 1946 I had left my home in Bristol to spend two years in the USA. Since then I had visited nearly every one of the states, gained two degrees, married a beautiful American and settled, for the time being, in the sunlit climes of California. It sounded like the script of a Hollywood movie, except it was all true and every day I thanked God for my good fortune. We set up home in San Francisco and eulogies could be penned in praise of the warm, sunny, wintry days – for which the very name of California is a by-word the world over – throughout which there was never a frost to mar the ever-blooming white arum lilies and scarlet hibiscus. They grew with the vigour of weeds in everybody's garden. Moreover, in all the year there were only three days of rain. It was wonderful!

During this time I renewed a friendship with Ron Goldman,

who had been a fellow student for the Ministry at Lancashire College in Manchester. There is no question that Ron and I had been most fortunate young men. In our youth we had both felt a call to the Ministry of the Church. It was not a sudden conversion, but the gradual development of a feeling that we were being marked out for the full-time service of God. At length, this sense of vocation so gripped and dominated us that we were both impelled to give up our secular occupations and apply to become students at a Free Church Theological College.

Before any aspirant to the ministry can get into one of these places much preliminary work has to be done. A whole sheaf of recommendations must somehow be acquired from one's own church, minister, friends, and much harder, from the local district committee, and the county committee of one's denomination. Sermons and life histories must be submitted, searching questions must be answered. Also, various examinations have to be taken at different stages. However, after running the gauntlet of such hazards, Ron and I were admitted – jubilant that our complete lack of financial resource was no bar to being accepted, but also sobered by the thought that academically we should have to start from the bottom.

Perhaps it was brilliance in Ron and bulldog tenacity in me which enabled us to wrestle successfully with Greek and Hebrew and the multifarious other subjects which were calculated to prepare young men for a parish ministry. As a matter of fact, many think that they more effectively produce budding theologians than young pastors equipped to be spiritual leaders among ordinary people.

Ron, like me, had decided to come out to the United States, with his newly-acquired Scottish wife, for post-graduate study. They had come twelve months after my own arrival, but they were to stay for only one year. This meant that both he and I would be returning to England about the same time in order to find a pastorate and to be ordained. And so the wheels of destiny began to turn which carried us home, where our lives were to be moulded and shaped in ways beyond imagining. It was as though a great hand began to move us toward England, and a half-forgotten, grimy Northern town, blinkering our sight and preventing any prospect but this meeting falling beneath our forward gaze.

Maybe it was the sumptuous civilization of the new world, and the bustling prosperity of institutional religion there, which caused us to think about our future work perhaps a little more than most ministers who stand on the threshold of their career. Neither of us had escaped temptations to stay in America. Already, one or two churches, charmed by the English accent, had dangled prospects before us more attractive than any could hope to achieve back home. To all of them we said "No", explaining that the main objective of our being in America was to acquire insights and experience that would enable us the more effectively to help resuscitate churches in England.

Resuscitate is the wrong word, here used advisedly. If the causes of the phenomenal decline in the power and influence of organized religion in England over the last 100 years are still in dispute, its dismal reality is agreed to by all. Our own denomination had lost tens of thousands of members, hundreds of ministers and an average of fifty churches a year – and all this despite an increasing population. The war, just ended, had wreaked further damage and destruction, buildings had been blitzed, and in many areas, congregations decimated. In hundreds of churches in the industrial North it was not only our own denomination, but historic Protestantism as a whole, which for years had been fighting a rearguard action, not against positive hostility, but against sheer indifference.

Ron and I knew about all this. Since we were on the verge of involvement in such a situation with the prospect of spending the rest of our working lives in it, how could we not be filled with alarm and dismay? We were also brought up sharply by the fact that many able ministers, trying to exist on salaries that were less than those being paid to a street cleaner or a steel works labourer, were struggling with heroic consecration to revivify churches in still populous neighbourhoods that had been reduced to a mere shadow of their former strength. But in most cases they were struggling in vain, and the disillusionment of some had driven them to other jobs. Again, this was especially true of the industrial areas where the ground was stonier, the battle fiercer, and the visible rewards almost non-existent.

Not for the ministers in these regions, or indeed anywhere in England, was there any paid secretarial help such as was enjoyed by their counterparts in the States. All office and office-boy work was done by themselves. In many cases they were also expected to run the church organisations themselves, superintend the Sunday school as well as preach two full length sermons at different services on the Sunday, and conduct a mid-week service. This was to say nothing of pastoral visitation and the community responsibilities laid upon ministers. Even today, life tends to become a rat race, a treadmill, a prison. Even if mental and physical health remain unimpaired, the hard-pressed parson becomes so bogged down in the routine jobs of the ministry that he never has time to sit down and think, to feel the winds of God blowing through his soul, and thus become receptive to a new vision of adventurous possibilities. If this near-miracle did happen, the vice-like grip of routine demands might be enough to prevent the implementation of it. How much worse the situation becomes when the minister is responsible not just for one church, but two or three with all the burden of work that that implies.

I gave much thought to this and so did Ron. Then one day, quite independently of each other, there flashed into our minds the realisation that if two ministers could work together at one church, what exciting opportunities for new endeavour there might be! What mutual support and encouragement would come to both! How much extra time and energy could be made available for creative experiments in church life! Who could tell what the concentrated effort and devotion of two trained men lavished upon one church might not achieve! Such an arrangement, while commonplace in America was virtually unheard of in England. It might mean the beginning of new life there, not only for one church but, in the end, for many.

Letters passed between us about this. In the spring of 1948 he and his wife, Jean, came to see Dolores and me in San Francisco.

"Would you be prepared to go in with me?" he asked. It was an inevitable question, and I had no doubt about the answer.

"Yes", I said. "But it would depend upon our being able to find the right church. Were you thinking about an industrial area?"

"That's right – anywhere like that."

"If only we could get a place which had more or less gone to pot but where there was still a chance to make a go of it."

"Of course," Ron replied. "But we don't want a church that has obviously outlived its day and ought to be closed anyway; it's got to have people living near it, so that it can become a community centre, and that presupposes large premises."

"Right, but where on earth do you think we could find a place that will fulfil all those conditions *and* can afford to pay two full-time salaries, even though they won't amount to very much?"

I was rather startled at Ron's answer. "I don't think there will be much difficulty about the money side of it," he said. "There's a wealthy church in Hinsdale that is willing to back this for two years as an overseas mission's project."

It was tremendous news. Apparently, one Sunday while preaching there, Ron had spoken casually to the officials about the possibility of a co-ministry with someone in 'darkest England'. Their imaginative sympathy had been aroused and a tentative offer had been made by them to pay half the salary of each minister for two years until we could build the church up to the point of being able itself to afford both stipends. The question of what would happen if we failed to do this was vaguely at the back of our minds, but neither of us seriously entertained such a possibility.

Full of glowing excitement we wrote off to the General Secretary of our denomination about the plan, which we hoped would meet with approval. It was also suggested that he introduce us to a church whose needs demanded the concentrated kind of ministry that we envisioned. Back came an enthusiastic letter assuring us that the denomination would give full backing, and promising to link us up, if possible, with a suitable church. He nevertheless advised us to make sure that the Hinsdale offer was a firm one before going ahead.

We did not have to wait long before receiving our first contact with Masbro' Chapel. The Honorary Secretary wrote to us and conveyed the following information. Masbro' Independent Chapel was situated in Rotherham, a northern England town of about 85,000 people, one of the most heavily industrialized in the whole of Great Britain. The chapel, founded in 1760 and with seating accommodation for 1,200, had been full of people and vibrant with life during the golden 'Age of Victorian Dissent' and just after, but now, like so many others, had fallen on evil days. Nevertheless there were great opportunities. Thousands of working people still lived in the surrounding neighbourhood, and the church, while poor in funds, was rich in premises, these being the most extensive of any church in Rotherham.

This seemed just the kind of place, and subsequent correspondence resulted in the church deciding to suspend further search for a minister until Ron and I could arrive home the following December. From private sources we learnt one or two other facts about the situation, one being that the former minister had resigned eighteen months before, having failed to make any effective impact. Disillusionment had taken him right out of the ministry into another profession, prompting him to say, "I wouldn't go back into it for the world; wish I had given up ten years ago!" At any rate he had given it up, and left behind him a church which was not only very weak, but also divided. There were those who regarded him almost as a candidate for sainthood, and were angered over his enforced departure, but others felt he should have moved out long before. Since then a number of men had been considered for the pastorate. Some wanted to come but were not asked; others were asked but declined the invitation.

This was the position of the church fellowship when Ron and I declared our willingness to go and talk with them immediately upon our arrival in England the following December.

And so, with excitement and no small measure of trepidation, Dolores and I began our long journey back to the east coast, in early September, on board the San Francisco Bay ferryboat. It was not easy to say goodbye to our well-loved city, and all our friends in the Fellowship Church of All People and elsewhere.

The first lap, after a few days in Sacramento and Colusa, was 900 miles up through the states of Oregon and Washington to Seattle and the coast of British Colombia. Here we climbed 6,500 feet up the 14,000 foot high Mount Rainier. There, with the Goldmans, we had a snowball fight on one of the great glaciers, yet the heat was so intense we had to take off our shirts – the men, that is.

From this extreme north-west corner of the continent, we took the train 1,000 miles through almost virgin forested mountain country of northern Idaho and Montana. The train – North Coast Limited – was the most luxurious we had ever travelled on, and glided with the smoothness of a billiard ball over the rails. This particular lap took twenty-seven hours. The next was another 900 miles from Billings, Montana, through Wyoming to southern Colorado. As far as could be seen, the state of Wyoming was absolutely barren. A hundred miles would sometimes go by without the appearance of a single habitation. Then the train would stop at a place called, for example, Chief Grey Bull, and still there would be nothing as far as the eye could see.

So the journey went on, and we went to see a great number of Dolores' relatives and friends. This was a task, or rather a pleasure, which took us to widely separated places, such as Des Moines, Iowa, Chicago, Wisconsin, Illinois, Detroit, Philadelphia, Washington and so on. We stayed a few days in the capital and, like two tourists, made it our business to go to the White House, the Capitol, the National Museum of Art, Washington Monument, Jefferson Memorial, Lincoln Memorial, the State Department, and others. While there we went to see several embassies, including, of course, the British. On 16th Street I was so bold as to take a photograph of the Soviet Embassy, being closely watched all the time by a guard inside the embassy door. But the venture was ill-fated, for strangely enough the picture never came out.

After a trip into New England our 7,000-mile journey (zigzag fashion) came to an end. Though we had been staying in New York, with solicitous and charming friends, the final three or four weeks had been somewhat exasperating. The Queen Elizabeth was due to sail on 24 November, but a strike in New York delayed her; several times we were almost on our way – first to Quebec, then to Halifax, Nova Scotia. But the strike was settled, and those miserable British Isles generated for themselves a murk of impenetrable opaqueness which kept the ship in dock another few days.

In the meantime, a poem was written by Elden Mills, Minister of Hartford United Church of Christ, to commemorate our departure from the United States:

Life is made sweet by the friends we have made
And the things which in common we share.
We want to live on not because of ourselves
But because of the people who care.
It's in giving and doing for somebody else
On this all life's splendour depends.
And the joys of this life, when you've summed it all up,
Are found in the making of friends.
I've been asked to write a poem
To be read to you folks today,
Regarding a much loved couple
As we realise they are going away.
We knew them not when they came here,
Nor what kind of pastor we'd face,
Only that Herb and Gen were off to Britain,
And the preacher from there would take his place.

Reverend and Mrs. Grant, we were to know them,
From Bristol, in England somewhere
But Dolores and Cyril, we love you
And want you to know that we care.
Cyril, you've dipped in the waves in our ocean,
Sipped tea at our tables, we're glad,
Even shown pictures of yourself bending iron
To show off the muscles you had.
Dolores, your charm and your kindness
Captured us right from the start
And your thoughtfulness and warm understanding
Will leave a fond spot in our heart.
You have cycled the streets of our City,
Toured the geysers and Monterey by the sea,
And from our strange leaking tea pots
We hope you have enjoyed our tea.
I guess what we'd really be saying
If each one had something to say,
Is that we'll cherish your friendship always
Even when you are oceans away.
So may God be with you on your journey
With good wishes through sunshine and rain
We won't say "Good-bye" as you're leaving,
Just "so long, and please come back again."

The journey across the Atlantic took six weeks and because it was winter there wasn't the occasion for lounging on deck and basking in the sun, as I had done two years previously on my maiden voyage across. Nonetheless, it was a pleasant trip made even more delightful by our stewardess, a kind and solicitous young woman whose affability led us into frequent conversation with her. During a few pleasantries on our way up to lunch one morning, she suddenly said, "And where are you going to settle in England?"

"Rotherham," we replied.

At this, despite the ability which her practice as stewardess must have given her of hiding unpleasant thoughts and feelings, her smiling face changed into one of obvious dismay and she merely said, "Oh." The matter was never referred to again, but it seemed that from that moment she regarded us only with pity and foreboding. If we had revealed to her the kind of vocation we intended to pursue in Rotherham, and the sort of achievements we envisaged for ourselves over the next few years, she might even have wept secretly for us.

We were very far from weeping ourselves, in spite of the fact that the great liner was heaving and shuddering under the impact of fifty-foot waves, our appetites were still enormous, and we also had unimpaired capacity for enjoying the prospect of Rotherham – though we did so from the vantage point of abysmal ignorance.

Chapter Seven

A Mission to the North

So, on a raw wet day in January 1949, my friend Ron Goldman and I sat in a train steaming north from London. We were both in our twenties and for eight years had been preparing ourselves for what we hoped was going to be our life-long work. Now the train was taking us to Rotherham, a nondescript, smoky industrial town where our career was destined to begin.

As the carriage wheels rattled over the rail joints for hour after hour there must have been much conversation between us, but I cannot remember it. Did we discuss with a tinge of apprehension the unknown life into which we were rushing at seventy miles an hour? If so, I do not recall it. Did we tremble at the frightful enormity of the tasks which would face us in this northern town which neither of us had visited before?

But the trivia associated with big occasions are often remembered when more important happenings fade from the mind. Our first journey to Rotherham was no exception, and the following incident is still clear in my mind.

About twenty minutes from our destination, my friend suddenly said to me, "You surely aren't going to wear that tie for our arrival?!"

It was meant to be a rhetorical question. Nevertheless I replied, "Why not, what's the matter with it?"

He shrieked. "It's a horror, that's all."

I had vertical stripes of white and red in the flamboyant American style, but was convinced, and returned, "Nonsense, it's a beautiful tie."

A WAAF who was listening and looking at us out of the corner of her eye was thereupon appealed to by Ron. "Is that the right sort of tie to wear for an interview for a job?" he asked vehemently, requiring the answer, "No".

She gave it – almost. "It's...it's..." She did not finish the sentence, but her hesitancy was eloquent. I had always believed the majority to be right in any situation – an opinion I was to alter radically in the next few years.

Time was getting short, so I protested no more and changed the offending neck tie for one of navy blue with polka dots. Everyone was happy including the wives who, though they took no part in the dispute, showed by their faces whose side they were on.

Almost at once after this, the train began to slow down. I went from the hot compartment into the corridor and peered through the steamy windows. The swiftly falling dusk and the rain had almost blotted out the landscape, but not quite. I could see that we were running parallel with a long line of tall chimneys from which smoke and flames were pouring and from which arose a dense mass of factory buildings whose black shapes stretched away into the night. Fascinated, I gazed for a few moments, then turning to the others said, in a half-cracked voice, "This must be Rotherham."

Streets of jumbled, soot-begrimed houses drifted slowly past the carriage window, and my mind roved back to the very different kind of environment with which we had been surrounded six weeks before. Interspersed with the closely packed houses and factories were streets still lit by the greenish-yellow glow of gas lamps which flickered in the smoky air; it looked rather like a Hollywood set depicting Victorian England.

The station itself had suffered from years of neglect occasioned by the war. Paint had peeled off the iron pillars and woodwork. Most of the glass had disappeared from the roof. Yet as we stepped down on the platform this impression of decay was in a moment dispelled by a smart, middle-aged man who walked briskly up and announced that if we were Grant and Goldman, then he was Charlie Chislett, the church treasurer. "Welcome to Rotherham," he said.

We suitably responded to the greeting, and Ron excused himself in order to obtain from the guard's van, at the end of the train, a variety of suitcases, rucksacks, boxes and holdalls etc. In fact we had fourteen pieces between us and much of it belonged to the Goldmans who were on their way home to Scotland having docked at Southampton on the Queen Mary only a few days before. Our host was taken aback at this grand array, and his natural suavity for a moment was shaken.

"What a lot of luggage you have," he said. I have never been allowed to forget the incongruity of my reply which was, "Don't worry yourself about that; we'll give you a hand with it." And, we did!

It was no doubt most inappropriate and inauspicious that on our way to Mr Chislett's home, we were so inwardly convulsed by laughter that it required willpower to prevent ourselves from guffawing aloud.

Over ten years later, in a meeting to mark my final departure from Rotherham this was the first of the episodes which prompted the church secretary to describe me as the most unorthodox minister the church had ever had. But there were reasons too which make me very glad that none of us could see what those future years were going to hold as we drove away from Rotherham station on that dismal January evening.

Charlie Chislett lived on the west side of the town from the railway, very much on 'the right side of the tracks'. It was like going from Bethnal Green to Ashtead or East River to White Plains. The 'age of the common man' in England had not resulted in class desegregation here any more than it had in Russia or America.

The area of Rotherham in which Chislett and his family lived was carefully defined and unofficially set apart for those who could afford to pay for top quality, from the fine young trees which adorned the grounds to the best undercut of beef which rested in its silver dish on the antique serving table.

Though not ostentatious, the Chislett residence and everything about it was of impeccable taste. Valuable ivories and a Steinway Grand in the lounge, exotic trophies brought back from extensive foreign travel, a 'den' full of cinematograph equipment, in addition to sumptuous wall-to-wall carpets everywhere except in the dining room which was strictly Old English, convinced us that we had come to stay with people of substance. Moreover, from the beautifully landscaped gardens which surrounded the house on every side, it was possible, by standing on tiptoe, to see miles away on the horizon the rim of a solitary chimney stack. For anyone in the neighbourhood of Rotherham to be able to live on a piece of land, from which such an unusual view was possible, bespoke affluence indeed. No ordinary bank official could sustain such gracious living without large private resources to supplement his salary, and the Chisletts were possessed of these.

But wealth was the least valuable of their assets. They were people of boundless goodwill who were always on watch to help as many individuals and worthy causes as possible, and they did it without condescension, self-righteousness, or any desire for return. They also struck us as the most un-snobbish people we had ever met.

After a dinner of chicken and strawberries we discovered that Mr Chislett was an expert producer of cinema travelogues in colour. His skill in this hobby had earned him a place on Foyle's Lecture List and taken him to many parts of the country for film lectures. Fees derived from these were always given to charity, and a variety of organisations had benefited to the extent of thousands of pounds. Nonetheless, his chief interest was the church over whose uncertain finances he presided as treasurer. This splendid man was also one of the eight lay preachers belonging to the chapel and the sermons he preached from time to time in the surrounding churches revealed him not only as a person of insight and sure knowledge, but also as one still keenly seeking further light and truth.

Mrs Chislett, stout and freshly-coloured, startled us at first by her 'north country' bluntness. Most people are too polite or afraid to utter their uncensored thoughts, but not Mrs Chislett. She described the tie I had been persuaded to change for our arrival the previous day as "the most ghastly thing I have ever seen". She declared me to be a "selfish oaf" (quite rightly) when I chose the biggest boiled egg in the rack at breakfast time. But these things were said with such good humour, despite the flashing eyes, that the idiosyncrasy was almost endearing.

We drove down to the chapel next morning for the Sunday services. We were conscious that for the whole weekend, we were 'on trial', that our every movement, gesture, word, was being carefully scrutinized by the church and its officials who naturally wanted to be sure, if they invited us to accept the pastorate, we were going to be the right men. But this task was not only theirs, it was also ours. We had to be as certain as it was possible to be that we were suited to meet the needs of this particular type of church. In other words, raising the question to its highest and ultimately its only legitimate level, did we feel called by God to begin our ministry here?

Suddenly Masbro' Chapel came into view. What a shock it was to see it for the first time! When our host said, "That's it," we thought for a moment he was joking.

Nevertheless our impression upon seeing this edifice for the first time as we bumped over the cobbled street between the rows of dismal four-room houses, was one of profound disappointment, indeed, almost of horror. Built of red brick which had aged and blackened with the years, it was like a large square box with two rows of tiny windows, one above the other, along one side of the wall. Ancillary buildings, just as dirty and nondescript, were built on to the brick box and stretched away for some distance up the road. On one side of the church, which was built at an angle of about forty degrees from the main road, was an enclosed space containing a few grave stones and one stunted tree. Opposing winds blew all the accumulated filth and rubbish of the neighbourhood into this space and it was sometimes used as a dumping ground for heavier refuse such as milk bottles.

It did not look like a church; it looked very much like a factory, and this is what many people thought it was, a product of the devout, yet aesthetically insensitive, eighteenth-century dissenters, to whom beauty in architecture was symbolic of the Devil. The inside of the church however, presented a pleasing contrast. Serried ranks of pitch pine pews sparkled with rose-red varnish, and were crowded together as thickly as in a theatre auditorium, both on the ground floor and the gallery which ran round the entire building on four different levels. Moreover, every seat and pew were so placed that they were directly facing the pulpit. Ron and I were amused to see that it could be entered from either side by means of curved staircases – a very convenient feature for a co-ministry!

While one of us presided at the morning service, the other preached, and these roles were reversed in the evening. This was always our method. Neither of us was really nervous on this occasion. Certainly we were not paralysed by the feeling that we were on trial. Perhaps it was partly because we knew there were other churches to which we could go if the Masbro' people did not want us, and it was also true that the officials, still being without a minister after searching two years for one, had turned their disappointment into something like desperation.

At the close of morning service, when Ron and I reached the vestibule to shake hands with departing worshippers, a little girl who had got there first held out a bag of sweets to me. "Have one," she said, "and would you like to take one for the other priest?" This incident added a trifle to our growing impression that Masbro' was a considerate and generous church. Already the treasurer had handed us £20 to cover weekend expenses – which were non-existent apart from the few shillings train fare from London. This was an enormously high fee, and more than matched the open-handedness of American churches.

Next day one of the senior deacons, a well-to-do wholesale fruit merchant, drove the four of us about the town and neighbouring countryside so that we should be under no illusion as to the kind of area it was. We saw miles of jumbled industrial plant, juxtaposed with blocks of ancient terraced houses crumbling away beneath the perpetual pall of factory smoke and fumes. But this was not the only kind of scenery. A few miles beyond Rotherham there thrived a green and pleasant countryside of rolling hills; yet even this landscape was blemished here and there by the pit gear of a coal mine with its mountain heap of slag and red-brick clusters of colliers' homes.

Afternoon tea at the deacon's house was a friendly and informal affair. Sugar was severely rationed in those days, as was nearly every other commodity. While at tea, Ron and I were thoughtless enough to take heaped spoonfuls of it, and our wives immediately rebuked us, giving us a look in which there was more severity than jest. The Hobkinsons laughingly waved it away as being of no consequence. But Dolores and Jean kept fixing us with their fierce gaze. Sidney Hobkinson noticed this and when the time came for us to have another cup of tea, this sixty-five year old stalwart of the church, seized the sugar basin while the others were talking, slid quietly off his chair and surreptitiously crawled on hands and knees round the back of the settee, suddenly bobbing up by the side of us before we knew what had happened. He silently indicated we were to take as much sugar as we wanted. And we did!

In the evening, at the Chislett's home, Ron and I met the whole body of deacons – sixteen in all – to discuss the matter of our settlement in the pastorate. These men and women upon whom the leadership of the church devolved were drawn from almost every social class. The managing director sat side by side with the steelworker. The poor had an equal voice with the rich. There was a school teacher, a housewife, a carpenter, a fruit merchant, an optician, two bank officials, and one or two other company directors.

"What kind of ministry do you envisage?" one of them asked.

I replied, "We should like you first to realize that we are not looking for an easy time. Our aim would be to increase the strength of the church, to build it up spiritually and in numbers, to recruit new members from the immediate neighbourhood, and to make the church a community centre as it once was."

"But what specifically do you intend to do?" someone broke in.

Ron explained that we had not completely worked this out but that the size of the premises, containing five large halls and other rooms, would make it possible to expand the organizations and to introduce new ones, especially for the young people.

"Unless we can get young people in their teens," he said, "there's not much chance of getting them afterwards." There were murmurs of assent to this.

"Ours will be a ministry concentrating on preaching and pastoral work of course," I went on. "But a co-ministry such as ours would be an almost unique happening in this country and the church must be prepared to absorb new ideas and to try new methods."

"Such as what?" the fruit merchant asked in a gentle voice.

"Well," said Ron, "for one thing we should like to put up an occasional play in church to take the place of the Sunday evening sermon. For another, we may be going into the public houses."

There was no reply to this, and altogether the deacons turned out to be a very uncommunicative group. As no one said anything, I followed it up. "Mr Goldman, of course, also hopes that his special psychological training will come in useful. He has a Master's Degree in it and some experience in pastoral counselling in cases of peculiar difficulty. There must be many people both inside the church and out whose lives are in such a mess that they would be more than eager for help from a Christian counsellor if only they knew where to go for one. Mr Goldman feels that he would like to set aside most afternoons of the week for this. Quite apart from helping people for its own sake, one of its results might be to draw them within the church. Do you think that members would approve this aspect of the ministry?"

All were sure they would.

I was not going to mention anything about my own secret hope of specialisation, but Ron did.

"It should also be pointed out," he said, "that Mr Grant has written a thesis in the field of Social Ethics and is particularly interested in the relationship of the church to industry. If only we could do something in local factories to bring Christian influence to bear upon the inter-play between management and labour, for example – at any rate this is what we should like to attempt."

A small, gimlet-eyed man then cleared his throat and gave every indication that he was going to deliver himself of a weighty announcement. This man was Ernest Twigg, the secretary and director of a large and prosperous boiler-making firm, who had been a life-long member of Masbro' Chapel. But he was so angered at the way in which the previous minister had been 'kicked out', as he put it, that he resigned all offices including his place on the diaconate. Tonight he was the only non-deacon present and had been especially invited as a tribute to his wise judgement and long experience of chapel affairs.

"In view of what Mr Grant and Mr Goldman have just said," he began, "I think a completely frank word about the chapel should be spoken. I have nothing against these specialised activities that they have mentioned, but we must ask whether they are going to build up the church and do it fairly quickly. This is the first consideration, because we are in most desperate need. Mr Grant and Mr Goldman have seen our vast premises; they are aware that thousands of people live in the neighbourhood of the church, and some of you have emphasised the scope that this would give them.

"Nevertheless, I feel most strongly that we should be guilty of deceit if we did not admit that the church is in a very bad way. It would not be exaggerating to say that its life hangs by the merest thread. According to the year book our membership is over 270, but take twenty people out of the church – any twenty – and you will kill it. That's the situation we are in. And you all know it as well as I do. Somebody had to make it plain. Masbro' Chapel was a great and thriving church once, but the glory has departed, and we should be inviting these two young men to come here under false pretences if we failed to make that absolutely clear."

This vehement and solemn speech, which rang with authority and was patently sincere, acted like a douche of cold water upon the meeting. Deacons were stunned by it for a moment and sat in silence. We ourselves did not know what to say, although the facts came as no surprise to us.

Charlie Chislett finally spoke in confirmation of them. "I'm quite sure," he said, with sweet reasonableness, "that Mr Grant and Mr Goldman understand exactly what the position is, and of course, they will have to decide in the light of it whether they want to come. If two ministers together cannot lift us out of our malaise, what hope is there that it could be done by only one man?"

Later in the meeting, another aspect of our settlement was discussed. The treasurer said that the funds of the church did not allow them to contemplate such a co-ministry unless the help from Hinsdale church in America was absolutely assured. This assurance we were able to give. Mr Chislett then explained how our salaries would be made up. Although we knew that life would not be easy on such a small pittance, especially for our wives, we were also aware that there were plenty of ministers struggling to bring up families on a much smaller stipend.

In the morning we were driven to the station to catch a train for our respective homes. On the platform, Mr Chislett said – for the second time – "We are having a specially-called church meeting on Wednesday about the pastorate; I'll telegraph you immediately afterwards."

As the train pulled out, I was certain we should see Rotherham again, but deep in my soul, felt the faintest rising of hope that we wouldn't. However, within days we each received the following telegram:

HAPPY TO REPORT UNANIMOUS REQUEST BY CHURCH THAT YOU SHOULD BE INVITED TO UNDERTAKE JOINT PASTORATE. LETTER FOLLOWING. *Frank Wragg*

It had been readily agreed between us before leaving Rotherham that if we received a unanimous or near-unanimous call, it should be accepted. Ron and I were anxious to be settled and were led to believe that Masbro's needs and opportunities fitted in well with the kind of co-ministry envisaged. We were sure that God was directing us to this church, although when it actually came to the point of sending off our reply, accepting 'the call', we both felt a bit weak-kneed. Not far beneath the surface-impression of high confidence which we gave and which was all other people saw, were those fears and hesitations which are normal in men taking their final and irrevocable step toward the ministry.

We were not engulfed by these problems, but they were enough to cause an underlying mental discomfort and nervousness in the days before our ordination. It was akin to the stage fright experienced even by world famous artistes as they wait in the wings.

The double ordination and induction in March 1949 was an event which roused widespread interest. News items appeared in national daily newspapers, with small headlines such as 'Marshal Aid for a Congregational Church' and 'US Aid an Experiment'. More detailed accounts were written up in the religious and local press, while an announcement concerning the ordination was given over the radio in the BBC northern news.

Those taking part in the service included a highly placed lay woman from New York to represent the American churches of our denomination. It was in fact the same Angel of Light who had come so unexpectedly to my study four years before. There was also a former minister of the church who had himself commenced his ministry at Masbro' following postgraduate work at Union Seminary, New York. But the most important and impressive person present was old Dr Berry – the denomination's elder statesman. The career of this tall, white-haired and perpetually beaming cleric had recently been climaxed in his appointment to a post which made him the acknowledged world-wide leader of our denomination.

Nearly everyone who could claim the slightest connection with Masbro' Chapel wanted to be at this unique event in the church's long history. Backsliders whose membership had lapsed years before crept sheepishly back and came in from curiosity to see what all the fuss was about at, "t'old chapel." In addition, representatives of all the other churches in the town, except the Roman Catholic, crowded in. Though no one sat in the enormous gallery which held most of the total seating accommodation, the ground floor was comfortably filled with about four hundred people.

This mood was undoubtedly fostered by the hymns. 'Praise My Soul the King of Heaven' was followed by 'Lord, Speak to Me, That I May Speak in Living Echoes of Thy Tone', and finally a little known hymn by Judson Savage was peculiarly apposite:

What purpose burns within our hearts?
That we together here should stand
Pledging each other mutual vows
And ready hand to join in hand.

Addresses from the rostrum were replete with a variety of wisdom and advice. Members were warned that they had to be, "receptive to new ideas, new methods, new adventures" and were, incidentally, reminded that, "Mrs Grant is 6,000 miles away from her home and her people are the most hospitable in the world; strive to match that fact with your kindness and consideration."

As the ordinands, Ron and I each delivered a very short address and as is usual on such occasions, gave a brief biographical sketch, speaking of the years of spiritual awakening and preparing which had thus led to ordination.

My own address reached a quiet peroration as follows:

"My aim in this sacred task is quite simply to do it as well as I know how, and to be a good minister of Jesus Christ.

"I shall do my best to uphold the true Christian fellowship of this

106

church, to develop its vitality and outlook, to increase its membership, and to make of it a family of consecrated people in whose corporate life those outside will be eager to join. I shall strive to help this church realise its destiny, as an instrument of God for the salvation of mankind.

"My trust is that it shall make an influential witness in this community through you who belong to it, for the reason that your religion is rich in the power of God's goodness and love. Therefore in a world distracted and broken, full of fears and distrust, let us, as ministers and people, go forward with resolution believing that the blessed God and Father of men has yet great things to accomplish through us his children."

The act of ordination was performed by the Rev John Smith – the denominational Superintendent of the Province in which Masbro' Chapel was situated.

We were given the option of receiving from him the 'laying-on-of-hands', but this we refused, first because we could see no particular efficacy in it, and secondly on the grounds that it might be regarded as having something to do with the Anglican and Roman Catholic belief in the doctrine of Apostolic Succession. Later on, circumstances resulted in a drastic change of our opinion about this.

A minor, but deeply satisfying aspect of the service for me personally was that my father, a brilliant and sensitive musician, had been given the opportunity of presiding at the organ. For him too, years of hopeful anticipation culminated in this event, but it also happened to be a culmination for him in more than that sense, for in three months he was dead.

Serious matters are not usually without their lighter side, and this was true of the ordination. Immediately following it, participants adjourned for coffee and biscuits. These were served in one of the numerous halls which led off from the back of the church. Dr Berry and Mrs Demarest came out of the chapel well behind the others and were uncertain about which room to enter. "I think this is it," she said, turning a handle, and ushering the old doctor into the ladies' toilet! Much amused, he became mockingly superior all at once, and declared that he never liked to contradict a lady, but all along had been much more certain than she as to the room the others were in. Whereupon after a few sure steps he flung open a door nearby which, to their joint astonishment, led into the gentlemen's toilet! Eventually an escort had to be sent out to bring them in.

After this incident, one of the first jobs we caused to be done was the clear marking of rooms, halls, and all other places. Even so one minister, who had been making periodic visits to the church for thirty years, told us that he had not yet learnt to find his way about.

Only one small disappointment marred the exhilaration of the day. The whole service was wire-recorded so that in future years we would the more easily be able to relive the experience of its meaning. But that same night as the wire was being rewound prior to our hearing the first play-back, it suddenly leapt off the reel and ended up as a chaotic mass on the floor. In this condition it was sent back to the manufacturers never to be heard of again.

A work of fiction might deal melodramatically with such a happening, perhaps marking it as an ill omen. But the thought that it really might be, never crossed our minds. On the other hand we were struck by the strange juxtaposition of our ordination photograph on the front page of a local newspaper with a headline which said, 'ANOTHER EXPLOSION: HOUSES SHOOK AT GREASEBROUGH'. Was it childish to be amused at this? Was it immature to wish that the church, if not we ourselves, could begin to cause explosions and shake homes as it had often done in history, and surely must do again, breaking up old habit-patterns to create new-born people, or else be forced to acknowledge itself an irrelevancy in the modern world?

This was the mood in which our ministry began, and these the stark alternatives as we saw them.

Now, the next task occupying our minds was finding somewhere to live. Once upon a time the minister of Masbro' Chapel had lived in a twenty-room mansion standing in its own grounds – Orchard House. But that was in the early part of the twentieth century when the minister had social prestige, a large family and, at the same time, a large income to provide for both.

Consequently, when the four of us came in January 1949 there was no accommodation. The former minister had rented a house from an old member of the church, but after relinquishing the pastorate in 1947, and entering a different profession, he continued to reside in the town and occupy the house. So now the church was faced with the need to purchase not one but two houses at the worst possible time, when its own finances were strained, and also when the post-war shortage of houses had sent prices rocketing.

While this matter was being considered it was arranged for us to occupy together, a small furnished four-room house about one mile from the church, at a rental of three and a half guineas a week. The owner, an army officer on tour of duty in Egypt, had taken out the best furniture and replaced it with junk. Wear and tear by former tenants had not improved these 'appointments' and when the Goldmans got into bed on the first night they found to their dismay that its springs touched the floor. They subsequently took the mattress off the bed and slept on the floor, which was slightly more comfortable. Our room was so small that the gas fire on the wall could not be lit without the danger of setting the bed clothes on fire. But such disadvantages were offset by having blackcurrants and gooseberries in the garden. The church had done the best it could for us in a town so overcrowded that some families had to live in one room and thousands with their in-laws.

Before realising how small a house it was that we were coming to, both we and the Goldmans arranged for numerous articles of furniture and books to be brought from various points of former residence. During the day, separate loads came from Birmingham, Bristol, London and Scotland. Somehow it had to be got in and crammed into tiny rooms with the rest, although we were able to store some of it in an unused garage. This facility was granted to us by people who were struck by the way in which we stood helpless and aghast before the mounds of furniture dumped in the driveway. Nevertheless much of it still had to be fitted into our own number15. After working feverishly all day to accommodate this constantly arriving bric-a-brac, we got ready for bed and marvelled that here was still room to take our clothes off.

Just then, about 11pm the door bell rang. A burly man in working clothes stood outside.

"Is the name Grant?" he asked.

"Yes."

"Then there's a load of furniture here from Manchester."

I reeled. The others listening did something similar. I had forgotten all about this. It was the contents of my study; there was a large desk, carpets, two easy chairs, various soft furnishings and over a thousand books with their bookcases. It all had to be unloaded and some attempt made to get it under cover. We asked no more than that. The premises already resembled those of an eccentric second-hand dealer who has bought so much over the years and sold so little that he can't move in his own shop.

Four months later, the church at last found a suitable house that was for sale at £1,850. It was fifty years old, of red brick, and pleasantly situated near a park on the residential side of Rotherham. This house, No 34, was purchased. Plans were made for furniture to be stored there for the time being.

In July when the tenancy of No 15 was up, the Goldmans went off on a month's holiday to the Pyrenees, while Dolores and I were given temporary accommodation in a church member's home. We could not go to No 34 as legal formalities had not yet been completed. During this time my father became ill and died, so that both before and after his death it was necessary to make several 320-mile round-trip journeys on family business.

Almost as soon as Ron had returned we departed for a holiday in Paris and other places on the continent, but in the meanwhile the church had been able to buy a second house. After being away all one day with the choir on its annual outing, Dolores and I, upon our return were confronted by the information that all within a few hours this house had become available and that an immediate decision had had to be taken. They hoped we would agree with what had been done.

Next day was Sunday, and after church one of the deacons drove us up to see number 51. The house was not unlike number 34, just acquired, but it did not look so desirable. A sixty-year-old red-bricked, semi-detached, unprepossessing in appearance, it had ten rooms on four floors and a tiny garden. But there was one unique feature, an ancient monstrosity of a shower built over the lower end of the bath and fitted with quarter-inch plate glass panels. Water came in fierce jets, not only from above but also like a hail of grape-shot from the holes bored the top to the bottom of the four supporting tubular steel uprights. The various handles and knobs at the side of the thing, to control output, resembled the bridge of a battleship, and when going full pelt it shook and heaved as though seized with convulsions, shooting almost as much water on the floor as in the bath.

Despite this fascinating contrivance for getting oneself clean, we did not much care for the house, nor on second thoughts, did the Goldmans, Jean declaring privately that she could not live in it.

However, the church had entered into negotiations for the purchase and that was that. Yet in accordance with our wishes and at some inconvenience to themselves, they tried to resell it at once, but in spite of wide advertisements could find no buyer. Surprisingly enough, number 51 was a more expensive house than number 34 and the two of them together cost the church nearly £4,000.

The big question now was, "Who should live in which?" Both of us wanted number 34, and neither number 51. Eventually we came to the conclusion that the fairest way to decide was by lot. So we did this by pulling pieces of paper out of a hat. Needless to say, the few moments it took were highly charged with emotion. The Goldmans picked number 34, so that Dolores and I were left with number 51. They were delighted for themselves and sorry for us; we were glad for them but chagrined at having lost the more desirable house of the two.

In the event, our disappointment was short-lived, and during the next ten years we never once regretted the fate which had forced us into a house we would not have freely chosen to live in. But in fact, more than once, we were moved to thank God for the many facets of joy which otherwise would never have come to us.

Chapter Eight

A Chequered History of Masbro' Chapel

One evening, more than 200 years ago, a group of swashbuckling youths swaggered up the narrow alley of Bridgegate on their way to the Nag's Head Tavern. They were an irresponsible and disruptive element in the Rotherham's life. But no more so than their modern counterparts who roam our cities with ugly weapons to slash and rob the unwary.

No record is left to us of the criminal exploits of this particular group of eighteenth century Teddy boys, but it is known that they very often spent drunken hours in the Nag's Head, and that at least on one occasion amused themselves in a very remarkable way.

These were the days of evangelical revival when John Wesley was riding all over Britain on horseback and preaching with unimaginable power to great throngs of people. As the result, thousands were swept into a life transforming experience of Christ, and not only by Wesley, but also by the 'Golden Voiced' George Whitefield. These two visited Rotherham more than a dozen times between them from 1752 to 1758, always preaching in the open air, and it was not unusual for them to be in danger of their lives while riding to fulfil engagements in the town. Among those who baited the two evangelists were the Nag's Head toughs, sneering and cynical. During an evening's carousel at the tavern, they would recount with malicious delight their attempts at opposition and violence.

On the night in question, however, having grown tired of this, they hit upon the notion of mimicking the great preachers. One by one they mounted a table, opened the Bible, picked a text at random, and delivered a blasphemous parody of the preaching they had heard. Leering and slobbering discourses were given by three of the youths in turn accompanied by ribald comment, and drunken caterwaulings. Moreover, amid the revelry, wagers were laid upon the best performer.

The fourth competitor was John Thorpe a ringleader of the group. "I shall beat you all," he cried. So having been helped onto the table he stood there unsteadily while the Bible was handed up to him. Leafing through it for a text, there suddenly came into his sight the words from Luke's Gospel, 'Except ye repent ye shall all likewise perish'. His companions waited for the unholy mouthings to begin, but this did not happen. John Thorpe stood transfixed, with his gaze riveted to the text. In a moment of time some mighty convulsion of the spirit surged within him, overwhelming instantly and forever the drunkard, the blasphemer and the criminal, flooding his soul with so vivid an awareness of God that he seemed to be brought directly into the Divine Presence. It was the Damascus Road experience all over again. By that mysterious alchemy dispensed only by God Himself, John Thorpe there and then became a new personality, a converted soul, and from that day lived under the compulsion of Christ.

After a few moments, possessed now by irresistible insights, he began to preach and expatiate on the text. An eyewitness declared, "In a flash he was favoured with a clear view of his subject and divided his discourse more like a Divine who had been accustomed to speak on portions of scripture than like one, who never so much as thought on religious topics except for the purpose of ridicule."

"If ever I preached in my life by the assistance of the Spirit of God," John Thorpe exclaimed in later years, "It was at that time." His companions listened in terrified silence, and when the sermon was finished he strode out of the Nag's Head without saying another word, and left them sitting stunned in their chairs. Unfortunately no one recorded whether this strange happening had any permanent effect upon them, but John Thorpe himself became a lay preacher, first under Wesley, then owing to a theological dispute, under Whitfield, the Congregationalist. Eventually he was ordained and invited to accept the pastorate at Masbro' Independent Chapel when it was founded in 1760.

For two hundred years before this, arising directly out of the Reformation, Congregationalism had been growing in numbers and influence despite cruel persecutions and the heavy burden of social and political disabilities imposed upon it. Those who openly dissented from the beliefs and practices of the Church of England were at one time hanged for refusing to conform. Others, in despair at the prospect of ever winning religious liberty in England crossed the sea to found a new society and became known as the Pilgrim Fathers.

In Old England the Toleration Act of 1689 protected Nonconformists from physical cruelty, but left un-repealed the discriminatory laws which forbade to them normal participation in the life of the community. Nevertheless, Congregational, Baptist churches and others sprang into being throughout the country, and made their most spectacular advance together with Methodism, during the eighteenth and nineteenth centuries.

Congregationalism became established at Rotherham comparatively late in the day, in fact, not until two hundred years after the first post Reformation Congregational churches had made their appearance in the southern half of England.

Rotherham Congregationalism discovered powerful allies in a rich and influential family of iron masters who became the founders and chief supporters of the chapel. It was in the Walker Foundry that one of their clerks, Thomas Paine wrote his famous book, *The Age of Reason* – an attack upon obscurantist Biblical interpretation of that day. The iron works at Masbro' produced great wealth for the Walkers, and their countrywide fame culminated in the manufacture of the Southwark Bridge over the Thames in London.

But their riches were devoted to philanthropy. Samuel Walker celebrated the growing prosperity of the business by erecting a day school so that the children of the neighbourhood might receive some education. It was in this building that Masbro' Chapel was formed in 1760 by the covenanting together of sixteen members. Two years later Samuel Walker paid for the erection of a church, but so rapidly did the fellowship grow under the leadership of Rev John Thorpe that in 1778 the original building was torn down to make way for a much larger one, and this too was paid for by the famous ironmaster. Following John Thorpe's death, the Rev Thomas Grove, a student at Oxford was invited to the pastorate. It is typical of the times that though destined for Holy Orders in the Church of England, he was expelled from the university for, 'reading and expounding the Scriptures and for praying extempore'. During his fifteen years ministry 172 members were added to the church roll, but eventually, perceiving signs of neglect of duty among adherents, he became discouraged and resigned. Two pressing invitations to return were sent to him without result.

This was a time of swift and vigorous advance for Nonconformity in the north of England, and the decision was taken to establish a college in Rotherham for the training of Congregational ministers. The importance of such a college was enhanced by the fact that Nonconformists were automatically debarred from becoming students at either of the two universities. As soon as the decision was known, Joshua Walker, Samuel's son, who worthily followed in his father's footsteps, offered to defray the entire cost. The college was built only a few hundred yards up the road from Masbro' Chapel in the same quiet rural surroundings. This college was demolished after a fire in 1874, being succeeded by a new one of magnificent proportions on the other side of town. However, only twelve years afterwards this second college was removed from Rotherham altogether to be amalgamated with another in the same county and its beautiful buildings, set in spacious grounds, provided a majestic home for the Rotherham grammar school.

But in 1795, the opening of the Rotherham Dissenting Academy, as it was called, added to the growing prestige and influence of Nonconformity in northern England. To match the importance of the event, a distinguished and learned minister, Dr Edward Williams, was invited to come from the famous Carr's Lane Church in Birmingham, not only to be the first principal of the college, but the new minister of Masbro' Chapel as well – an arrangement long carried on by subsequent principals.

A man of exceptional talents and industry Edward Williams left behind him a momentous record. Two of his students later held respectively the secretary-ship of the London Missionary Society and the British and Foreign Bible Society. In fact his was a large share in the formation of the London Missionary Society, and the honour fell to him to give the charge to the first missionaries it sent overseas. He also wrote numerous theological and metaphysical works. Upon his death in 1813 the coffin was deposited in a vault beneath the pulpit.

Up to this time Masbro' Chapel was the only Congregational church for miles around, but so enthusiastic were the dissenters of those days that every Sunday they would walk into town from outlying districts, covering as much as twenty miles there and back. These ardent souls brought food for the day with them, picnicked in the surrounding fields and attended all the services that were held. But during these years Nonconformist cells began to spring up in villages outside the town, as one after another they became centres of the mining industry. Sometimes, new churches were established by the initiative and help of the Masbro' Chapel minister and its members. During 150 years the old chapel has brought into being no less than fifteen other Congregational churches and a sixteenth was opened in 1958, which quickly became the most vigorous of them all.

After the death of Dr Williams, a successor of energetic and scholarly ministers, several of whom were Doctors of Divinity and later principals of other colleges, gave such able leadership that the congregation grew apace and the premises had to be enlarged both in 1830 and 1860.

In the mid nineteenth century Masbro' Chapel was not yet surrounded on all sides by blocks of dreary dwellings; its peace was not made hideous by the roar of main road traffic constantly agitating and polluting the dirty air; it did not yet look out on a scene of increasing dereliction and decay. The founders could never have foreseen such developments of course, but probably believed that if the chapel were built half a mile up the hill from the town centre it would forever be surrounded by trees and fields, thus affording its worshippers not only the spiritual tonic of Godly worship on Sundays, but also the health giving sights and sounds of nature as they journeyed to and fro.

The Walker family built themselves a splendid mansion not far from the chapel which for many years stood in the midst of their orchards and vineries. This fact is perpetuated in the names of two streets which almost adjoin the chapel yard, while the old college has given its name to the busy main road running alongside the building itself.

Throughout its two hundred years Masbro' was the spiritual home of local notabilities and the well-to-do as well as the lesser lights. When Ron and I arrived, there were people still alive who could remember the halcyon days when prominent and wealthy members drove up every Sunday morning with their families in sparkling carriage and pair. Frock coats and top hats were *de rigeur* then, with black lace and flying feathers for the ladies. This weekly arrival at church of such elegance was a sight anticipated and enjoyed by the neighbourhood, whose less favoured inhabitants watched from behind front room curtains or, more crudely, with their arms folded, standing on their doorstep.

A special room was set apart for footmen, drivers and other servants and the opportunity was given for refreshing themselves with beer and beef during the service. If they wished of course they were at liberty to attend public worship with their masters and mistresses, but not sit in the same pew or even in the same part of the church. Class segregation was an unwritten law, but one rigidly observed in

Victorian England, and it applied to all relationships whether within or outside the church. It was unthinkable that though God might look upon all men as equal the principle should be carried so far as to allow no distinction between master and servants in their worship of the Deity. Therefore downstairs was reserved for masters while servants were relegated to the gallery. Times had changed and class consciousness in 1950s England was less extreme, but the old idea still persisted that the ground floor and gallery of Masbro' Chapel represented two levels of social achievement.

In 1865 a dispute arose, which centred round the person of the minister, the Rev Isaac Vaughan. So violent was it that a number of members withdrew, together with the minister, and formed another Congregational church. Within two years they had collected sufficient funds to erect a building just off the centre of town and less than a mile from Masbro' itself. This neo-gothic structure with its tall slender spire was as beautiful as Masbro' Chapel was ugly; but the Rev Isaac Vaughan never preached there – he died before the opening day. The malcontents pretentiously called their new cause the 'Rotherham Congregational Church'. It began life with a great flourish, but was overtaken ninety years later by a fate so bizarre that it would have been beyond the wildest imaginings of its original members.

Masbro' Chapel itself soon recovered from their unhappy exodus. It became so thriving and its people so full of eager enthusiasm that missions and Sunday schools were started in neighbouring slums. Also in 1901 another new church was founded further up the hill, about a mile away in a pleasant and growing suburb known as Kimberworth. Tribute is due to the amazing strength and regenerative life of the church at this time that although no less than 142 Masbro' members voluntarily transferred their allegiance to the new Kimberworth chapel, thus guaranteeing it a good start, this loss was made up within two or three years. Indeed it was so much more than made up that in 1906, the church could proudly claim to have 561 members on the roll – more than at any time before or since.

This was the Golden Age of Nonconformist power and influence. The churches of dissent were full and prosperous, numbering many thousands up and down the country. In most local communities they counted for something, and were centres not only for the worship of God but also for the acquisition of moral culture and the expression of Christian fellowship. Moreover, in nearly every town prominent citizens considered it a privilege to call themselves Nonconformists.

Their political counterpart lay in the Liberal Party which received almost one hundred per cent support from them. In 1906 they reached the topmost height of political power for the general election of that year was made memorable by a Liberal victory of unprecedented proportions. During the next few years the free churches virtually ruled Parliament, and the occupants of famous pulpits in London could be sure that their Sunday pronouncements on matters of public concern would be taken notice of during the Monday morning Cabinet meeting at Number Ten, Downing Street.

Such was the happy situation of Nonconformity in years prior to the First World War. But though it could not be known at the time, Congregationalism had already reached the crest of the swelling tide and was thence forth to ebb gently away into the direction of obscurity – and this is still a continuing process. Never again was there to be so overwhelming a political victory as in 1906, and the great Liberal Party itself – the Free Church mouthpiece in Parliament – was to be reduced at length to a mere six members. Never again was the membership of Masbro' Chapel to stand as high as 561. And indeed, from that year the decline set in which persisted, with occasional checks, to the present day.

The general upheaval of life caused by two world wars, quite apart from the number killed in them, had a deleterious effect on faith; it did much to break the church-going habit, and resulted in decimated congregations. Never were such congregations seen in Masbro' Chapel after the First World War as before, and their size after the Second World War was never as great as in the years prior to 1914. The church, it seemed, was slipping toward extinction, and this was true of many more. Every so often a new minister would come, fresh for the fray. The novelty of new ideas, new leadership, would take hold and produce a burst of enthusiasm. Some of the uncommitted would take the decisive step, while a few people entirely outside the church would be drawn in and the membership would rise. But then before long the backward slide would once more become apparent, and the general life of the church would sink into stale inertia. All this would happen until, becoming tired of it all, or suffering a nervous breakdown or even succumbing to disillusionment, the minister left for another church or some other profession. Then the process would begin all over again. But at the commencement of each successive ministry the initial advance became harder to make and was of a smaller extent than its predecessors, while the subsequent decline became ever more precipitous.

Such had been the unhappy pattern of Masbro' Chapel's existence for many years prior to our acceptance of the pastorate in January 1949.

Was this racked and weakened fellowship in its death-throes? Some were sure of it and spoke of having the church closed. But our own question was quite different and our policy exactly the reverse. Was it possible through our ministry not merely to give a blood transfusion but cure the disease? Under the aegis of God and the compulsion of Christ we were determined to try.

Chapter Nine

Finding Our Feet

During our first few weeks in Rotherham there were plenty of eager people to tell us not only about the chapel and its great days, but also about the town itself, of which, in spite of its grim appearance, they were obviously proud.

Did we know the Romans had a town here 1,500 years ago? And that the excavations had brought to light fragments of beautiful villas and a temple as well as all kinds of containers and utensils? Did we know of the remarkable possibility that soldiers might have seen Jesus die because they were on duty in Jerusalem at the time, were later transferred to the fort which guarded the Roman settlement at Rotherham, now forever buried beneath the sprawling mass of the steelworks?

Up to the middle of the eighteenth century Rotherham itself was little more than a small town with a cattle market. Then the Industrial Revolution broke upon England, and spread like a black rash over the countryside, especially in those parts where coal was discovered. Rotherham turned out to be sitting on top of one of the most extensive coalfields in Europe. Within the next hundred years dozens of mines were sunk nearby and the close proximity of iron ore deposits made it an ideal place for the manufacture of iron and steel products.

Within a few decades the quiet and peaceful town whose antique beauty had shone like a gem set within wooded hills and valleys was gone forever. In 1949 official figures showed that every month thirty-six tons of soot per square mile descended upon the area. In 1952 housewives complained of having to do their washing two or three times.

The whole area suffered severely in the Great Depression. Community soup kitchens saved thousands of unemployed from virtual starvation. The church distributed food parcels and second-hand clothing. And many unemployed were rescued from boredom and crumbling morale by the minister of Masbro' Chapel, who made part of the church premises available for boot repairing and other handicrafts, with equipment supplied by the church.

In 1949 however and afterwards, in keeping with the rest of England, Rotherham was a town of great prosperity. Out of a population of 85,000, no less than 20,000 men were engaged in the coal mines or the steelworks, all of them earning good, and some, fabulous wages.

Such prosperity contrasted very oddly with the kind of houses in which most workers were compelled to live. The older parts of the town, those built prior to the First World War, consisted of dingy four roomed terraced houses laid out in long identical blocks squeezed as closely together and as near the factory as possible. Thousands had been quickly erected during the rapid industrial expansion of the nineteenth century by the wealthy ironmasters who were obsessed with a desire to get labour at cut-price rates and who therefore saw to it that the housing provided was as cheap and unpretentious as possible.

Masbro' Chapel was practically surrounded by houses of this dismal type. None of them had bathrooms or indoor sanitation; all were heated in winter by open hearth coal fires, and some were still lit by gas burners. Very few had gardens either front or back but shared a small stone yard with their neighbours at the end of which stood toilets incapable of being lit or warmed. Backyards were reached by means of a tunnel-like passage running through from the road between every four or five houses.

In 1949 the first post-war estates were already beginning to be built by the Corporation in an attempt to catch up on the war-years when no houses at all were built. Overcrowding was desperate, and occasionally even a family of six was compelled to live in one room. While such a situation existed, whole streets of wretched property already condemned as being unfit for human habitation had to remain standing and occupied. Much of this was near Masbro' Chapel. Some was better than others of course, but it is no exaggeration to say that ninety per cent of the chaotic mass of habitable, or at any rate inhabited homes, which hemmed in the chapel on every side were miserably outdated.

Before the matter of our own living accommodation had been decided, we seriously suggested to the deacons the possibility of our settling in the neighbourhood of the church instead of far from it, as all the ministers had done for many years. The deacons would have none of it. They resolutely refused to consider the notion that there could be any kind of dignity or spiritual advantage for the ministers of Masbro' Chapel to live in so alien and unpleasant a neighbourhood, even though it was the one in which the church was situated, and which presumably it existed to serve. It seems now that we too meekly acquiesced in this point of view. Perhaps we too easily tended to be won over by the argument of one or two deacons that to live in such a district would be too hard on our wives and also that for the church to purchase a house which, together with the rest, had such a poor expectation of life would be a very unwise investment.

What sort of people were they, these working folk who voluntarily segregated themselves in this downtown part of Rotherham? They were uncomplicated, uncultured, prosperous, house-proud, incurably sentimental, and always ready with unfailing benevolence to help those in trouble.

The vast majority of people in this run-down area of Rotherham had had no schooling beyond the age of fourteen, and never succeeded in passing the exams that would have qualified them for a grammar school. Most started work as a matter of course in the local steelworks, mines, or other industrial plant, settling there for the rest of their lives. During the 1950s wages were so high that at the end of the decade Harold Macmillan was prompted to tell the nation, "You've never had it so good."

During post-war years therefore, working people became the *nouveau riche* with money to spare. Very little was saved but much was spent on liquor, tobacco, and the football pools – practices heavily indulged in by all classes of society. For vast numbers of people 'pool's night' was on Thursday when the whole family got down to the business of forecasting the results of league football matches, together with the announcement of those results at Saturday teatime, and provided the only moments of excitement and drama in a very humdrum life. It was possible to win as much as £200,000 for two pence and some did. Many others got lesser fortunes; millions nothing.

But not all the surplus cash was thrown away. For the first time in their lives perhaps, workers were able to lavish money on their annual holidays. Not all went to the Butlin's holiday camps which provided artificial entertainment from morning to night; large numbers travelled to Austria, Italy, and Spain, etc. It was a significant commentary on the times that a Rotherham man, employed by the town as one of its rubbish collectors – a job which traditionally was among the lowest paid and which no one would take if he could get anything else – casually mentioned to me that for his previous annual holiday he had flown to Ireland for a fortnight with his wife and three children. This was a new era of prosperity indeed in which such things were possible.

Money was also spent on brightening and modernising, as far as practical, the dismal houses in which most working people lived. They were rented for ten to fifteen shillings a week, and owing to restrictions imposed by the government these rents had not been raised for many years. A majority of landlords, impoverished by such uneconomic returns could hardly afford to pay for urgent repairs, let alone repainting and modernisation. So this was done by some of their tenants. Of course it was much more eagerly undertaken by those who had bought their own homes, perhaps for the sum of £300 to £500.

The Yorkshire 'range', that ancient monstrosity which required black-leading nearly every day, and which gobbled up hundredweights of coal, was pulled out and replaced by a tiled fireplace of modern design. Old fashioned panelled doors were overlaid with smooth gaily painted plywood, and sometimes even a bedroom was cut in half for a bathtub.

Whatever could be done to improve the appearance of old property was done. The north country housewife was a proud woman and particularly proud of the house she lived in, however unprepossessing it looked. It was a rare wife who did not scrub and whiten her front step every day, and some would even do it to the stone window sills and the surrounds of the coal-shoot which were let into the pavement just under the front room window.

During the 1950s prosperity was also reflected in the number of luxury items for the home which were gradually acquired – flamboyant front room suites, TV sets, record players, washing machines, aluminium sink units, and even cars. Such a standard of living would have been beyond the wildest dreams of the working man's family prior to the Second World War. Compared with those days they were rich and wanted for nothing. In the field of material benefits they had achieved the full life, and appeared to be self-sufficient.

Such were some of the conditions of life for the people who lived in the neighbourhood of Masbro' Chapel. It was known as a working class district, but also one to which the church did not minister. Nevertheless, there were hundreds who called it, "Our Chapel" or with equal familiarity, "T'old Chapel"; yet except for certain personal emergencies, they did not attend it or share in its life in any way. With the supreme confidence of youth we believed it possible to change all this, and one of our prime objectives was to win for Christ through the church the allegiance of these people.

A wise minister once advised certain students on the eve of their ordination, "If you want to change anything in your churches, do it during the first twelve months." The implication of this comment is that congregations are never so ready to accept new ideas and to try new methods as at the beginning of a ministry. Minds closed against change start to open up a little, and even diehard conservatives who can no more justify customary ways of doing things than to say, "This is how it's always been done," become tinged with radicalism.

But it is all temporary, and before long attitudes harden and creative development is halted. Thus it was important to spend only a minimum of time in assessing the church's need for new activities and methods and to move as quickly as possible toward their introduction.

One day about three weeks after settling in, an opportunity suddenly came to bring Masbro' Chapel dramatically before the public. About this time international publicity was being given to the trial of fifteen Baptist pastors in Bulgaria who were charged with being in the pay of British and American intelligence services. Nearly everyone in the West assumed their innocence, and that the charge was both part of the Communist drive against organised religion.

Nevertheless, accurate information was difficult to get, since the only news reports of these men and their trial came from official Bulgarian sources. In the meantime, British papers were full of indignation that the God-fearing pastors had fallen victim to Communist treachery, and the feelings of the whole nation were outraged when it was eventually announced that they had all confessed their crimes and been sentenced to varying periods of imprisonment.

But was there the germ of possibility that the pastors were in some way guilty? Or on the other hand, was it a complete frame-up, with 'confessions' produced by brain-washing or physical torture? No one on this side of the Iron Curtain really knew, except perhaps one man.

My eye caught a paragraph about him in the *Manchester Guardian*. He was the Rev GB Chambers, vicar of Carbrook in Norfolk, and Anglican priest for forty-three years. He too had been concerned about the Bulgarian pastors and suddenly determined to fly out in a private capacity and attend their trial.

Baby Cyril with parents, grandparents and great-grandmother, 1919

Aged eighteen months, around 1921

Aged three, with a train built by his father

Aged four, outside his home in Sparkbrook, Birmingham

Aged six, in a school production of *The Pied Piper of Hamelin*

Aged seven, 1928

Aged eight, a choirboy at St Paul's CE Church, Margate

Christ Church School. Upper Department. May. 18th 1928

Cyril Grant is working in Std II.
He is a very keen boy + should soon
be a "top" school-boy.

His arithmetic is his weakest
subject, although not bad; but his
Reading, Recitation, + General knowledge.
are well above the average.

He is regular, punctual, willing +
most enthusiastic in all his work.

He will do credit to any school
he may attend.

Tom Norton.
(Head Teacher.)

Cyril's school report, 1928

In Bristol, aged seventeen

Cyril meets Queen Mary

Cyril and Dolores' wedding day, 1948

The Reverends Ron Goldman and Cyril Grant

'Signs of Hope', Masbro' Chapel as Cyril first found it

The forbidding exterior of Masbro' Chapel

The rear of Masbro' Chapel

The rather more interesting interior of Masbro' Chapel – Cyril is in the pulpit

Masbro' Chapel's organ

A radiant Dolores Grant, 1962

The idealistic young Minister – Cyril Grant, 1962

Commencement of Building - 1956.   Total cost : £45,000

HERRINGTHORPE CONGREGATIONAL CHURCH.

An illustration of how Herringthorpe Church may look

Farewell to the congregation of Herringthorpe Congregational church

Cyril as the Bearded Lady, Alderney Carnival, 1968

Just some of Cyril's hat collection

Cyril gives his final sermon as Minister of Redland Park Church, Bristol, in July 1984

The congregation of Redland Park Church celebrate Cyril's retirement, 1984

Cyril receives the Lord Mayor of Bristol's Medal in 2012

Cyril receives the MBE from the Princess Royal for his services to The Samaritans

Cyril poses with his MBE, 2012

Cyril with good friends Derek and Myra Jones following his MBE presentation, 2012

Cyril celebrates his MBE with his step-nieces in Windsor

Marking his achievements as Cyril 001 – the front cover of *Samaritans News*

The article in *Samaritans News*

Mary, Lady Fuller, Cyril and Hedley Funnell at the Dead Sea

Susie 264 and Maggie 20 with Cyril 001 on his 89th birthday

"Why don't we write and ask him to come up and speak to a meeting about it?" I suggested to Ron.

"Good idea. It could be a scoop if we could get him. He must be having hundreds of requests."

So, after obtaining the approval of our deacons we wrote to the Rev Chambers and within a few days, surprisingly received his acceptance.

But the following Thursday morning Ron and I returned home from some business in town to find Jean and Dolores in a state of semi-panic. "Mr Williams rushed round here on his bike this morning," they cried, "puffing and pedalling up the hill like a grampus – we thought he was going to have a heart attack." The Rev TJ Williams was minister of the self-styled Rotherham Congregational Church, a prim and proper, conventional type of minister, but a choice spirit for all that.

"Well, what did he want?" we asked.

"He says you must not let the vicar of Carbrook come, in fact he begs you not to let him come, and declares it will do you great damage."

"But why?" we broke in, now becoming alarmed.

"Because he is a Communist, that's why. In the *Christian World* this morning there is the report of a meeting he has been speaking at in London, and it gives a warning against him. He says it is quite clear that the pastors are guilty."

"Oh."

"Yes and Mr Williams came round as soon as he got the paper, so you could send off at once to stop the visit. It was very kind."

There was no doubt about that, but we were not convinced that we ought to take his advice.

Plans for the vicar's arrival were complete, and the meeting had been boldly advertised in several newspapers. It was surely not wise to cancel the arrangements on the ground that this man might put forward opinions with which we did not agree. Better by far, we thought, to let the vicar come and see what happened, even at the risk of having our own reputations tarnished.

So we did. He was an energetic, bald-headed little man, and as we rode on the top of the bus all the way from the station, kept on muttering under his breath such phrases as, "They are all seething underneath," and "It's a crying shame the way they're squeezed," and "The lid won't hold on much longer." All this presumably with reference to the thousands of workers at the various industrial plants we were passing.

In our letter to Mr Chambers we had hinted at a capacity audience of 1,000 people, but he did not seem to be as disappointed as we were, when only about eighty turned up. These included a few avowed Communists.

The vicar declared to the meeting that he went to Bulgaria to see what the religious situation was like.

As far as the pastors were concerned he declared his belief that they had been given a fair trial and were justly sentenced. "There is no such thing as religious persecution," he cried, "The clergy impressed that upon me."

Long before the end of the speech one could sense that the majority of the people present were hostile to Mr Chambers. At question time this was forcibly expressed and several charged him with being a Communist and therefore disqualified from being able to give an unbiased opinion of the trials.

The vicar did not specifically refute these charges and eventually brought upon himself the unexpected wrath of no less an antagonist than Mr Ernest Twigg. This was the same man who, on our first visit to Rotherham, had spoken to us so strongly in the deacons' meeting about the church's parlous condition. He was a devout Christian, but known also to possess a white-hot hatred of Communism.

This 'Chapel Stalwart', as the newspapers afterwards described him in flaring headlines, now rose to question the vicar. He did so with a face drained of colour and a voice thick with subdued rage.

Ernest Twigg shot out an arm toward the speaker, and with an attempt at self-control declared, "You ought to be ashamed of yourself, as a minister of religion, to condemn your brother ministers at this moment languishing in prison because of their religious and political beliefs. I cannot find words to express my abhorrence and disgust at the opinions you have put forward tonight and the fact that you have come to such a place as this to do it. I refuse to waste my time any longer listening to your pernicious drivel." With a great final crescendo of feeling he shouted out, "We shall fight Communism."

Thus ended, he heaved on his overcoat and strode out of the meeting. Everybody was electrified, and did not seem to want to ask any more questions after that. So when I formally thanked the speaker for coming and talking so frankly to us the audience dispersed.

One of the first repercussions of the 'Chambers Episode' as it came to be called, is that some people went about charging not only the vicar with being a Communist, but saying that we were as well. Members of the public were even overheard in buses referring to, "Masbro' Chapel and its two young Communist ministers." We met this by preaching a series of sermons on the theme, 'Christianity confronts Communism', which left our opposition in no doubt. In addition, we wrote to the press and specifically refuted the charges.

Ernest Twigg was not the only managing director who had gone to the meeting. There was another who stayed instead of walking out. He too was a church official and the head of an important glass firm. He said to us, "I didn't agree with the speaker, but think the meeting has been very worthwhile, and congratulate you on the initiative and imagination you have shown in arranging it."

Within two or three weeks of the 'Chambers Episode', another public meeting took place at Masbro' Chapel which was far more to the liking of the church people. Guest speaker was the Rev William Wallace, minister of the Methodist Victoria Hall in Sheffield. There were no Communists present this time as there had been in support of the vicar of Carbrook, in fact, nobody who was not associated with one or other of the sixty churches in Rotherham. William Wallace, a dynamic and straight forward speaker, harangued us eloquently and with humour about the 'Rotherham pagans'.

"Do you know," he asked, "that nine out of ten people in Rotherham are absolutely ignorant of what goes on inside a church?" We did not know it was as bad as that.

"The average person displays as much interest in church buildings as Christians display in public houses. The churches are dying today because they are isolated within their bricks and mortar."

"Get out among the pagan people of Rotherham with the Gospel. This is the challenge of our time. The church must attack. Only a revival of the Christian faith can save our country."

How much effect this address had upon the audience of respectable church-goers, apart from making them feel somewhat superior to the submerged nine-tenths, time would show.

As for Ron and me, we found our view reinforced that if the church fails to bring the impact of the Christian faith to bear upon those without, its continued existence cannot be justified. In fact the whole *raison d'etre* of the church is that it should 'go into the whole World'. When it becomes preoccupied with its own existence, to that extent it is moribund. As one of the leaders of our own denomination said, "We must go out, or we shall go out."

How many people were there of this calibre in Masbro' Chapel? Were we? How many were likely to catch the vision of the church reaching into every home in the community and there winning the allegiance of the family to the service of Christ? And even if they caught that vision, did it follow that the spiritual disciplines necessary to implement such an aim would be joyfully and continuously shouldered?

At the beginning of our ministry we were astonishingly naïve, yet one thing we were sure about is that the church must be made attractive enough for people to come to it. We hoped that a great many people would be drawn to Masbro' Chapel, hesitatingly and tentatively to begin with, perhaps out of curiosity to see what was being offered under the leadership of the new ministry. First impressions were likely to count for much.

Such was the theory on which we worked in the early days, and it seemed possible to make some immediate progress on this front.

Every church with a lovely building possesses an initial advantage, and it need not be a neo-Gothic structure for that. Some of the most aesthetically satisfying chapel buildings are those with well-proportioned but un-carved exteriors and straight lines that are symbolic of the simple faith which inspired them. Masbro' Chapel was meant to be one like this but its dingy surroundings, and with the dirt of eighteen decades upon its face, the structure was repellent. Some lapsed members and potential adherents excused themselves to friends by saying, "I'm not going down to that dirty old place in the slums." The appearance of the church was made worse by the fact that during 1939-1945, the eighteenth century spear-point railings which surrounded the tiny graveyard at the front had been compulsorily cut down to make munitions, leaving only the ugly stumps embedded in the low wall which was itself bulging outwards and threatening to collapse into the street.

So the sight that met worshippers plodding up from town, on the cracked pavements of College Road, was not a pretty one. And owing to a lack of funds the prospect could not immediately be improved.

We arranged for a large board to be erected behind the railing stumps informing the public that this gaunt edifice was in fact Masbro' Independent Chapel and that the services were at 10.45am and 6.30pm. And then instead of loading the board with useless information which appears on so many church notice boards, we asked for the following statement to be inscribed in gold on a black background: 'This is your community church and exists to serve you'. Such a declaration implying that the church was not a closed-shop of hymn-singers but was actually going to set itself out to give practical help to the people in the community was a rare sight on church notice boards.

People who turned a blind eye to the exterior of the building and came inside were pleasantly surprised at its newly decorated condition. The old pews now shone with varnish and the walls were resplendent in fresh fawn, as yet unsullied by dust. This was also true of the five main halls and the smaller rooms which, as money became available and the work expanded, had been erected at later dates. The whole vast suite of premises had been painted on the inside during 1948 at a cost which taxed the resources of the diminished congregation.

Furnishings were plain wooden tables and chairs. There were no soft furnishings such as curtains, tablecloths, pictures, nor any floor covering on the bare boards except in one room upstairs which was fitted with a now cracked and pattern-less square of lino. This was called the 'Ladies Room'.

All were spacious rooms, but austere and forbidding, like the Puritan conception of Christianity so devoutly held by our forefathers who had erected them. 'How was it possible', we wondered, 'to make these hard-looking interiors convey the impression that Christianity is not a religion of ugliness, but beauty, and not only one of discipline, but also of joy?'.

Ron and I looked long at the Ladies Room. On the wall over the open fireplace was a brass plaque dated 1894, 'In loving memory of Emma Clark by the girls of her Bible Class'. Running the length of another wall were coat hooks, and over in the corner was a door leading to the toilet.

It seemed intolerable to us that if these premises were to become the spiritual home of more and more people, as we hoped, there was no comfortable room where, in pleasant surroundings they could sit down and read and talk with their friends or just be quiet. We knew that in American churches there nearly always is such a room but in English ones, virtually never.

"What about making this into the church lounge?" Ron suggested to me about the Ladies Room. "It seems to be more suitable than any other."

I agreed but added, "We can't ask the church for any money to do it; they are committed up to the hilt. Why don't we make a general appeal for articles of furniture in good condition?" This seemed to be the only way. The scheme was explained to members of the congregation and contributions solicited.

The response was good. Several second-hand easy chairs came in, two people gave money which enabled us to buy a couple more, also a floor lamp and table lamp were donated. But the most lavish gift was from Ernest Twigg, chief of the boiler firm. He offered to pay for wall to wall carpets and curtains to all the windows as well as behind the two doors. This was munificence indeed, and by his special request the gift remained anonymous.

'The Lounge' as we renamed the Ladies Room provided, with its predominating colours of maroon and yellow, attractive and home-like surroundings ideal for discussion groups and social gatherings.

Next, we determined to have a suitable place in which people could come and talk with us if they wished for private conversation. But where could we take them? Only to the 'Minister's Vestry'; this was a tiny room at the side of the church – like something from the more dismal pages of Dickens.

About half as large as a normal living room, it had one naked light bulb hanging down from the ceiling. In one corner was a tall iron-black fireplace, which it seemed had not held hot coals for many years; in the other was a high-backed chair whose broken upholstery made sitting down impossible. Screens of black gauze covered the bottom half of the windows which, in conjunction with the mud splattered on the outside by main road traffic, dimmed the daylight. It seemed appropriate somehow that in this room, when we asked for the Baptismal Register, the Register of Deaths was handed to us, but not by mistake. The one had been made to serve for the other by crossing out 'date of deceased' and writing 'date of birth' above it.

"Whether or not people were suffering from spiritual depression when they came to see us in this room, they would be likely to suffer from it afterwards," we said to ourselves.

At our first monthly deacons' meeting we freely expressed the horror we felt about this room and within a week had received £35 from the glass firm director to refurbish it as we wished. This bought a carpet, two easy chairs, and a brightly tiled fireplace. A green and white table lamp replaced the naked ceiling light, and the final touch was added by Charles Chislett who gave us a water colour framed in light oak portraying the blue skies and white cottages of Connemara. Needless to say the black screens and old chair were taken down to be fed into the furnace and the windows cleaned on both sides. Now we had an interviewing room able to please rather than depress.

One other change was made. The portraits of former ministers – about fifteen of them, hanging in a massed formation round the walls, were all reduced to frames of one size, set into a polished mahogany case about thirty feet long, and displayed in the entrance vestibule, suitably captioned – ours among them by special request! This collection going back two hundred years became known as the 'Rogues' Gallery'. The whole display was paid for by a former mayor of Rotherham currently chairman of the town's Finance Committee. Though reared under the wing of Masbro' Chapel he had not attended any function there for years and always declined to resume his association with the church.

Nothing more could be done at the moment, we decided, to spruce up the appearance of the old place, heavily committed financially as it was. Structural disadvantages could never be overcome, but a good start had been made in turning one or two repellent aspects into pleasing and even attractive features. Yet these were the least important changes to be made.

Already existing in the church were two most effective uniformed organisations – the Girl Guides and the Boys' Brigade, staffed by competent and dedicated officers. But there were types of teenagers who were not attracted by the demands of loyalty, obedience and purposive work made by these groups, and for whom something else was needed.

Our answer was the Arrow Club. On Easter Bank Holiday, 1949, we rounded up about thirty young people and took them out walking into some beautiful hill country about fifteen miles away. Most of these were already associated with the church, and a few were in their late twenties, but none belonged to the uniformed organisations.

"What kind of activities were they hoping would be started for folk of their age?" we asked. "What sort of week-night programme did they think would attract other young folk into the church?"

Their answer was unequivocal. "A club," they said, "for games."

"Nothing else?" we asked.

"Yes, some dancing and a film now and again."

During the following weeks, with a group of selected youngsters an elaborate programme was drawn up for submission to the church. The premises were to be open on Monday, Tuesday, Wednesday, and Saturday, for billiards, badminton, and for table games in the lounge. In addition to the entrance fee of 2/6d a small charge was made for games, as for example 1/2d for each person for twenty minutes of table tennis. Moreover, a cricket and football team were to be formed. Membership of the club was open to all young people from the age of fifteen, and though it was not intended to exercise any compulsion, all members were expected to attend either morning or evening worship on Sundays. The committee of six – all church attenders – and we ourselves, thought this a reasonable expectation which avoided the smug exclusiveness of the closed club and the do-as-you-please attitude of the open one.

"We want a name that's going to fetch 'em in," seemed to be the general opinion, or as we ourselves more pompously put it, a 'distinctive and meaningful name'. After several now-forgotten suggestions, an equally un-remembered person – it may have been me or Ron or anybody – came up with 'Arrow Club'. It struck us all as having merit – a club directed to the target of Christian living. So it was adopted.

The other difficulty of finding money to purchase equipment was not so easily solved. There were already some badminton rackets and shuttlecocks packed away in a junk room, but not nearly enough. And there was a billiard table in the Institute Hall. But where were the pounds to come from for table tennis tables, football and cricket gear, etc? The church could not pay and it was beyond the immediate capability of club members. At last it was jubilantly discovered that the education committee of the town council might be prepared to make us a grant. The committee sometimes voted money to youth clubs if they could prove they were providing recreational or cultural amenities for the community. On our application form we promised to do this if only the committee was forthcoming with the money! They were. We applied for £100 and got it, thus being able to buy all the sports tackle needed. To supplement this, Charles Chislett, the bank official and church treasurer, gave a couple of netball posts.

The next job was to find volunteer adults to act as supervisors on club nights. An appeal to the congregation brought in one or two; Ron and I privately persuaded a few others – all men. Their task was to keep order during club hours from 7pm to 10pm, collect the small charge made for games and see that the premises were securely locked before slipping the keys into the caretaker's letter box about a quarter of a mile away. Thus all was made ready. There was no need to advertise the club's opening; word got around. Some teenagers came by invitation of the few already in the church, and a few wandered in by themselves. Soon there were about sixty – as many as we could handle.

One night a few weeks after the opening, a deputation came to me and asked, "Can't we have a canteen? There's nothing for us to do while we are waiting around for others to finish their games."

I pointed out the difficulties. "Of course it is a good idea," I said, "and I'll see what I can do, but you know how severely we are rationed, two ounces of tea a week, quarter pound of butter, half pound of sugar. The Ministry of Food is terribly tight-fisted about letting clubs like this have a special ration." They understood. But I applied to the local office of the ministry whose officials checked and rechecked the figures stated in my application, deliberated together, and finally allowed a small weekly ration of the above commodities and others. Every ounce had to be carefully accounted for in a book to be kept available for inspection at any time.

Again, volunteers had to be recruited to staff the canteen, and it was done by women of the church, all of whom strangely, belonged to a distinct type; they were in late middle age and came from working class homes. None of the church ladies higher up the social scale came forward to help.

Almost immediately after the club was opened it became necessary to have some administrative organisation. A 'council' was therefore selected, consisting of the two ministers, who sat ex-officio as joint presidents, a chairman – one of the older young men in his twenties who was also a lieutenant in the Boys' Brigade, a secretary and treasurer, plus four committee members, each of whom were responsible for a particular piece of work. One looked after equipment and another was in charge of team fixtures.

In its most thriving period, to come very soon, the club had teams each in the local table tennis, badminton and football leagues. During the summer tennis was played at reduced rates on a court in one of the town parks. Some members also joined the Masbro' Chapel cricket team which had now been revived after many years.

One night, nearly a year after our arrival in Rotherham, an official of the education committee from whom the club had got its hundred pounds, came in unexpectedly to see how things were going on. He saw the splendid equipment, surveyed the animated scene in three halls, beamed approvingly and said, "You are doing a grand job. This must be one of the best clubs in town."

Chapter Ten

The End of an Era

Though holding to the view that preaching was important, we also believed that other forms of presenting the Gospel could be equally effective. We therefore formed a small group called the Sanctuary Players, which enabled us occasionally to stage one act plays as a substitute for the sermon, especially at Easter and Christmas. Ron was usually in charge of these productions and made exacting demands on the performers. Great care was taken with lighting and staging, but the time and effort expended were well worth it. Plays usually proved to be a deep emotional experience for the congregation and were long remembered.

Only one received negative criticism. This was called the *Deathless World*, an Easter play whose theme suggested that without death, life would be robbed of its meaning.

We had not realised before how many people resent having to think about the subject of death, which they regard with horror, and try to keep it out of all conversation. Even of some Christians this is pitifully true. Therefore we were surprised that when this beautiful play was performed before a congregation of about two hundred one Palm Sunday evening, two people fainted and one walked out. Another declared with choking vehemence that she would never come to Masbro' Chapel again. But she was there the following Sunday!

The first play to be put on was *The Other Inn*, a modern counterpart of Mary and Joseph's search for accommodation in Bethlehem, portraying a homeless refugee couple about to become parents. The performance necessitated building up a stage and curtaining off some side pews. But it was in these very pews that there traditionally sat the two old Misses Milnes, retired, unmarried, school teachers in their mid-seventies. From such a vantage point, with their gimlet eyes, they could keep the whole congregation under constant surveillance as though it were a class of boys and girls. They noted who sat with whom, every new costume, coat or hat, and concentrated a baleful gaze upon any strangers present as much as to say, "And what brings you here?" The two sisters would carry on a hissing conversation with each other about these matters, and had been coming to Masbro' Chapel for so long that they could remember walking down College Road as little girls, picking primroses and violets from the fields on either side.

Just before the production of *The Other Inn* we went to them and explained that the pews in which they sat would be curtained off. Therefore for this one occasion would they mind sitting elsewhere?

They thought for a moment and then the larger boned and more masculine of the two said, "Mr Goldman, we've sat in this pew for fifty-three years and we really don't see why we should have to move out now."

They didn't, and remained stolidly behind the scenes for the whole of the service, hearing little and seeing nothing.

But progress won in the end because for subsequent performances they abandoned their customary places and sat with the congregation. Or perhaps it was because they could not for a second time bear to miss seeing who was there!

What was the reckoning for our ministry at Masbro' Chapel at the end of twelve months? The church was in good fettle and progress had undoubtedly been made. One sensed this to be the view of those who attended the annual meeting at the church in March 1950. There were about eighty-five of them and their mood, like ours, was one of sober confidence.

We all had something to be confident about. Nobody wanted to put it in these terms, but it looked as if the church had been pulled back from the abyss into which it had almost slithered. Reports from various departments spoke of a new zest and increased membership. Everyone was cheered to hear how splendidly the new organisation had done. Charles Chislett announced that his appeal at the beginning of 1949 for an increase of £800 (fifty-five per cent) in church giving had been successful. This was a phenomenal achievement as also was the £635 raised at the one-day Annual Sale of Work and Gift Day in November.

Yet it was Frank Wragg, the church secretary, who had the most encouraging things of all to say. "We have been pleased with the sermons preached by our two ministers and feel that no church could have had better ones consistently."

But Ron and I were not drawn into the danger of thinking the church could rest on its laurels; they would never be big enough for that. I myself spoke to the annual meeting as follows, "When we came to Masbro' last year at a difficult time, we could see years of hard and patient work ahead. What has been achieved so far should not lull us into thinking we can rest back and that those years of hard patient work are still not ahead."

After describing the coming year as "vital" in deciding whether the advances made so far were just a flash in the pan or the beginning of a long-term achievement, I finished as follows, "Will you therefore take it to be your personal ministry this year to make the work of our church more widely known and to enlarge the circle of our worship by bringing others into it?"

During 1950 especially, the church continued to grow in numbers. No less than forty-one adults were received into church membership that year 'upon profession of faith'. All of them attended the course of instruction given by the ministers. But not all who came to the classes were received into the church. When it came to the point of commitment some were honest enough to say they felt unable to meet some of the requirements; these were nearly always the obligation to be regular in attendance at public worship, church meetings and Holy Communion. Those who felt they could not give top priority to these fundamental responsibilities usually withdrew from the classes and thus saved us embarrassment.

But the fact about these new entrants which was really disturbing is that the great majority, though new to Masbro' Chapel, were not coming into a church for the first time. Moreover, they did not live in the surrounding neighbourhood, nor did they belong to the 'working class' strata in society. In other words, they were conventionally middle-class folk already disposed towards the church who at some time, had had a tenuous or even close association with it.

Of the small minority that belonged to the mass of working class people in the immediate neighbourhood of Masbro', all were teenage girls who were really not outsiders at all because they had been scholars of long-standing in the Sunday school. Therefore the church was making no appeal whatever to those thousands of families within its own parish who had never professed any interest in organised religion.

How to reach these? One way was to go and talk to them at home, which we did later on. Another was to go to public houses which many of them frequented. The public house makes its appeal to all classes of society and the social level of our district was such that nearly everyone gravitated to the public bar. They were the people we were after. Though Ron and I were not total abstainers, neither of us had ever been in a Rotherham public house, and we wondered how to get a start.

"There was that woman," I said, "whose dying mother I was asked to go and see down at College Road Inn. She seemed to be friendly enough. Why don't we talk to her about it?"

We did. "Do you think your customers would like us to come in on one Sunday night and conduct some community hymn singing? And what do you think their reaction would be to a prayer and a scripture reading?"

Her answer was unhesitating. "I am sure they wouldn't mind. In fact, I believe they would like it," she said. A couple of weeks later the visit took place and it was a great success. With Ron conducting and myself at the bar room piano, familiar hymns were sung with uninhibited gusto as customers laid their books on the beer-wet tables beside them (we had taken the precaution of bringing old ones!). One old chap disappointed at being out of it, explained that he could not join in as he had forgotten to bring his teeth! Some people were anxious to keep as mementoes the sheets we had had printed with the titles and numbers of suggested hymns. We allowed this, but when they also wanted them autographed, Ron half-humorously declared, "That will be half-a-crown," whereupon they were hastily drawn back.

One of the greatest attractions to people of this and all subsequent visits was our Masbro' choir mistress who we took with us. Her appointment six months before had been made at a time when the church was in despair at being unable to replace the organist/choirmaster who had resigned on the ground that he was not suited to the work. The two jobs were then separated and, although after great difficulty, the position of organist was filled, but six months of frantic searching failed to turn up anybody willing to become choirmaster. Then Sybil Bainbridge volunteered, and her offer was accepted, though not without some misgiving. She was a forty-one year-old good-looking woman of sizeable proportions and with a chequered career. The church people knew with what enthusiasm she had worked successively for spiritualism and Communism before abandoning both. She knew very little about conducting choirs but her almost overwhelmingly magnificent talent was that she could sing. Sir Hugh Allen, former director of the Royal College of Music, once described her as having, "the voice of the century." There is no question that Sybil Bainbridge contributed enormously to the appeal of our public house services. Her requested solos Ora *Pro Nobis*, *Abide with Me*, *The Holy City*, *Star of Bethlehem*, etc were in great demand and received vociferous applause.

Our initial visit to the College Road Inn particularly, resulted in wide publicity with reports and photographs appearing in several newspapers. The pub and the church represented two different worlds, each being supposed to be at enmity with the other, but here was an example of friendly fraternisation between the two and here were ministers of the church actually being welcomed into a public house to lead drinking people in the worship of God! – an almost unprecedented occurrence. This was news indeed.

But trouble was in store. No one at the church told us face to face that they did not look with favour upon the pub visits but one or two things were said behind our backs. One woman from a working class home thought the scheme a 'grand idea', but another, whose husband was a company director said, "It's a foolish waste of time; they would do better to concentrate on the church." Ernest Twigg, aggressively teetotal was against the visits on the ground that we did not use them as a golden opportunity to condemn the evils of drink.

But they provoked much more widespread criticism than this. The deputy president of the Rotherham and District Bank of Hope and Total Abstinence Union attacked our policy in a public speech, though without mentioning us by name. "If a minister holds religious services in a public house," he declared, "he is serving the cause of the brewer by advertising his place of business. The minister is also doing harm by making a difficulty with children who might get the impression that public houses are fit and proper places because the minister goes in them..."

These were feeble arguments, we thought, though we had no intention of replying to them. This was done by the local newspaper in a trenchant editorial. 'The Deputy President is striking an intemperate note on a subject which calls for tolerant thought and outlook. Let him look to the methods adopted by Our Lord Himself who had no scruples about the company He kept or where He went. We should have expected that total abstinence advocates would have looked upon public house evangelism as taking the fight into the enemy's lines."

The pub service always commanded a reverence among customers at least as genuine as that shown by church congregations. During the prayers there was no sound or movement except when newcomers pushed in through the street door without prior knowledge of what was taking place. Each one stopped dead in bewildered amazement to see sixty or seventy silent customers bent low in prayer over their beer, until in a moment they too were moved reverently to worship.

Finally, it must be said that the most bizarre and unforeseen result of our pub visits was unconnected with persons at all and concerned my own music copy of the hymn book. Prior to each service, it was placed upon a table in the bar while I leafed through to find hymns and tunes. These tables were sometimes wet with liquor and after a while I noticed that the pages were gradually soaking it up. Then I was more careful, but the damage was done and for a long time afterwards, when ever the gas fire in the vestry had been on too long or too high, fumes would rise from the hymn book on the table, with the result that the whole place smelled like a still!

Old and lonely people, often from quite a distance, were among those coming to Masbro' Chapel on Sunday nights. The aged and infirm were among the most consistently loyal members of the congregation, and their motives for church attendance were usually much higher than that of the old age pensioner who said, "Well it's somewhere warm to go to in winter." But so it was, and the winter nights were often wet and sometimes bitterly cold. The older folk were especially in mind when we thought how much people would like a cup of tea and a biscuit before starting out again for home. Moreover, they were of a generation whose Sunday evening delight after coming home from church had been hymns round the piano. Why not make this possible for them once again?

Thus the idea of a social hour, not just for old people, but for anyone who would like to come, was suggested to the deacons. It was accepted without reluctance and without enthusiasm, and met with that same reaction from the church meeting, apart from a very few.

One of these was Winnie Lee, a vigorous, sparkling eyed saint of a woman in her middle fifties who glowed with quiet Christian vitality. She earned her living as a highly skilled optician in Sheffield, but her real job in life was the church, to whose welfare she devoted herself with keenest enthusiasm. More than once she had had the chance to move out from the nearby depressing street where she lived, to a more modern house, which she could well afford in salubrious and healthy surroundings, but this was refused on the grounds that it would be too far away from the chapel. Miss Lee was a deacon, a leader of the Sunday morning Junior Church, and the Junior Department of the Sunday school, as well as being engaged in all sorts of unofficial and often furtive good works among those in the congregation. Eager to encourage and slow to criticise, she was always in the forefront of people volunteering to help with new endeavours and experiments, even though more overburdened with work than most. With it all Winnie Lee was the very reverse of being officious or overbearing; her grace of character and poise of bearing were things to be marvelled at. "I will do anything I can to help in the social hour," she said. And she did; taking her turn at providing the food and drink, and being present each fortnight when the social hour was held, to help with the preparation for it and the washing up afterwards.

Twenty or thirty people were usually present in the lounge, not all of them old. There they sat in front of the fire's leaping flames, sipping their tea, chatting with their friends, and afterwards singing the old familiar hymns.

Always a leading light at these social hours was Bert Bagnall, one of the town's leading fruit merchants. His black suit and polka-dot bow tie hardly seemed to go with a face that was so coarse and ugly, it might have belonged to a retired prize fighter. But Bert could get out in front and lead the folk in community singing as no one else could. He was a showman and he had the common touch, and gained much sympathy as well as applause by singing solos himself.

Although 1950 was a year of growth in church activities, of

increasing congregations and unabated enthusiasm on the part of the ministers, there occurred within that year certain events which boded ill for the future.

Though too 'progressive' for the liking of some, Ron and I were old fashioned and orthodox enough to believe that a church was not doing all it should unless some leadership were given in corporate Bible study.

The church was therefore prepared for the commencement of a course of Bible studies to be held each week by the ministers for an indefinite period. 'Adventures with the Bible' they were called, and that is just what we intended them to be. The series was to be based on Sir Frederick Kenyon's *How we got our Bible*, and Fosdick's *Guide to Understanding the Bible*. Ron and I took it in turns to preside at the meetings and lead the discussion.

But from the point of view of numbers the series was not a success. No more than six people ever came. These included two seventy-five year-old bachelor brothers, and Mr and Mrs Tennent, who soon withdrew on account of fundamentalist views.

But at first, before becoming aware of our 'heretical' tendencies they were enormously keen, especially Mr Tennent, who as it turned out afterwards, was most certainly touched with religious mania. He could conceive of no spare time having any value whatever which was not spent in reading the Bible, praying, or otherwise worshipping God. One Wednesday night he arrived in a sadder and more solemn mood than usual. "I asked a girl last Sunday to come to these classes," he said.

"Good," I replied, "What did she say?" I could see it was not anything satisfactory to poor Mr Tennent, for he was now the very personification of gloom.

"She said, 'I go to church three times a Sunday, teach in the Sunday school, have preparation class on Friday nights, come to the Arrow Club on Monday and Thursday, attend night school on Tuesday; so Wednesday is my pictures night'."

"So that was it?" I asked.

"Yes, I was shaken to the foundations; it was merely another proof to me that this generation is going straight to the dogs."

I knew better than to argue. The Tennents themselves were soon gone forever from 'Adventures with the Bible', and most of the others too, but not for the same reason, until we were down to two regulars. Rightly or wrongly, it was decided that this number did not merit the time spent in preparation and presentation, so the class was brought to an end. It had lasted just six weeks. Whatever reason people gave for non-attendance was hardly ever the true one, but it covered the widespread affliction of which they were half ashamed, and which can best be described as being 'not interested'.

The failure of 'Adventures with the Bible' occurred just about the time that the Men's Fellowship Forum took a decision of policy which might have justified those who thought that religious people are interested in everything except religion.

The committee of the forum had invited a Socialist, a Communist, and a Conservative to come and speak on Christianity and their respective political parties. Nobody seemed to mind the Socialist or Conservative politicians but there was an outcry against allowing a Communist even to come on church premises. The protest was led by that arch-enemy of Communists, Ernest Twigg, and the church secretary, Frank Wragg. They were not condemnatory of the ministers or the committee but the church meeting urged that no Communist should be given the opportunity of bringing propaganda into the church ever again. No vote was taken but there was obviously strong support for the view, some even suggesting that it would be better not to invite any political speakers at all to the forum. Ted Alderman, the president, promised that the whole matter would be considered at the next meeting of the committee.

When this took place a few weeks afterwards, we were dismayed to hear him suggest that all subjects of a political and religious nature be banned. As chairman I asked what support there was for this view but no one wanted to say anything except Fred Pugh, a rough speaking man of limited education but with a keen political consciousness who, with his wife and daughter, had astonished us all by drifting into the church some months before. He regarded the church as an instrument of 'social good', no more, no less, and saw the Men's Fellowship Forum especially in this light. Faithful attendance and volubility of speech more than anything else had got him elected to the committee.

"What madcap idea do ye think you're playin' at?" he asked, "Thee'll ruin the bloody thing. Are we like children wantin' little talks on pond life and such? Or grown men with guts? No wonder the church don't count for nowt, nor will it if ye bury ye heads in sand like this. A 'armless pleasant little Monday evening, that's what it will be, with everybody noddin' agreement about the beauties of Cornwall; but I tell 'ee, I won't have none of it."

I thanked Fred Pugh for his contribution and quickly asked Ted Alderman why he wanted to ban political and religious subjects, especially religious.

"Because they might lead to disagreement and bad feeling," he replied.

"Can you think of any speaker, except one, who has had this effect?"

No, he could not. "But you never know. These are the subjects that most quickly rouse people's prejudices."

"But surely," I interrupted, "we are wrong if we refuse to listen to other points of view just because we may not agree with them or because we are afraid our prejudices may be aroused, or even that we may lose control of ourselves in the heat of discussion; in any case, as Christians we should have no prejudices, but only firm convictions for which we can give a reason and which we are not frightened to defend in a spirit of calm discussion – and of course if we are not too bigoted it is always possible we may be able to learn something even from those we disagree with."

But it was all of no avail; they would not even defer the matter for further reflection, and it appeared that apart from Mr Pugh all were in favour of banning politics and religion from the forum.

The sad result is that although the programme continued to be of a high standard culturally, something vital was lacking; it was the stimulation of mind and spirit which come in being able to discuss matters of almost life and death importance to the world.

In the years to follow, the interest of members was maintained by a variety of subjects. Jack Jones, our Member of Parliament, came again to speak on 'Lawrence of Arabia' whose aide-de-camp he was in the First World War. 'The Beginnings of Rotherham Football Club' by a founder member, eighty years old; 'William Hogarth' by the Chief Librarian; 'Badger Watching at Night', and 'The Water Mains of Rotherham', were some of the stirring topics dished up, but no politics or religion. It was almost as though the local Communist Party had decided to forbid any discussion of politics or the British Medical Council of medicine at its meetings.

The foregoing failures, though disappointing, caused no despondency because the church was in good fettle and still on the upgrade. Once of some power and influence in Rotherham, the townspeople now began to note the arrival of its fortunes. This was partially due to newspaper publicity, some examples of which have already been mentioned. Also, articles about the church appeared in the religious press under such headlines as 'Co-ministry Breaks New Ground'.

As far as the income of the church was concerned, it rose fifty per cent in two years, from £1,038 to £1,569. The increase was due not only to the contribution of new members, but to the increased giving by others who knew that the Hinsdale Church gift of one salary for two years came to an end in 1951. Unless Masbro' had become sufficiently strong to raise both salaries by then, the co-ministry itself might come to an end as well. This was a spur indeed, for it is true to say that the great majority of people did not want to lose either of us and that everyone without exception feared the possibility that we should both depart together. But now that danger was passed. The church was in the remarkable position of being able to support us both, even if our monthly cheque came to no more than £28. No other church of our denomination in the north of England supported two ministers (though some of them would have been far more successful if only they could have done so). And in fact this ability belonged only to one or two wealthy congregations of enormous size in the south of England. For a church like Masbro' to do it, a church of departed glories, set obscurely within the decaying streets of a dingy industrial area whose people are notoriously indifferent to religion – this was something of a triumph.

And yet, though pleased with the progress made during our first two years, we did not feel it was anything to boast about, and were therefore acutely embarrassed at reading the following paragraph in a national religious weekly:

'It is just two years ago since the Rev RJ Goldman and the Rev CH Grant began their joint pastorate at Masbro', Rotherham. Arrangements have been made to celebrate this happy ministerial anniversary at the beginning of February. These two young men have not only done a great work in their church, but have made a valuable contribution to leadership and adventurous experiment in their work, and it is good to see how greatly their efforts have been rewarded...'

It should have been a happy period, despite some opposition. But storm clouds were gathering and one Sunday morning Masbro' Chapel's two ministers came down the curved red-carpeted stairs of the pulpit after closing the service. On this occasion, contrary to custom, they did not go into the vestibule to take leave of those dozen or so folk who had been in the congregation. Instead, Frank Wragg, Charles Chislett and Sidney Hobkinson, secretary, treasurer, and senior deacon respectively, were approached and asked to step into the vestry. There they sat uneasily on the blue velvet chairs while Ron conveyed to them in a few words his decision to resign.

"I feel," he said, "that the work of the church no longer justifies both of us being here. We have striven to bring new life and vitality to this fellowship and to build up its strength. These efforts have met with some success, but in the circumstances, I have come to the conclusion that things would be made easier for the church, especially from the financial viewpoint, if one of us were to move elsewhere. To be fair, I must also say that certain domestic considerations have led me to this decision and I should like you to know that I have been offered a post of Lecturer in Psychology and Social Studies at Westhill College, Birmingham."

As I sat there listening to this, it was difficult to know whether the three church officials were genuinely taken aback, or only seemed to be, having half-expected something of the kind to happen for some time.

"I take it," began the treasurer, "that you haven't called us together to discuss the question with you as to whether you should resign, but to present us with a *fait accompli*?"

"If you like to put it that way, yes."

"That makes it easier in a way of course, but I am sure that Mr Wragg and Mr Hobkinson will join me in saying how deeply sorry we are to hear it. Are you certain there is nothing we can do to persuade you to change your mind?"

"No, I took a long time to come to this decision, and my mind is definitely made up."

"What about Mr Grant?" ventured the senior deacon; the three of them turned to me. "Perhaps you haven't yet had time to think about your own position in the new circumstances, but we hope you won't follow Mr Goldman's footsteps."

My reply was immediate. "I have given much thought to this and I am ready to continue alone if the church wishes me to do so." Their unhappy faces brightened a little and I was assured that the church would be extremely relieved that one of us at least would be left.

Ron's decision to resign the Masbro' Chapel ministry was the climax to pressures which had been gradually building for some time both at the church and at home.

Jean Goldman, through no fault of her own, had found life in Rotherham hard to bear. To come from a pleasant house in the country to an old fashioned, hard-to-work manse in one of the ugliest and dirtiest towns in England would surely be an unpleasant exchange for anyone. And to give up a life of comfort with a wealthy father for one of penury with a £7 a week husband (even though he be dearly loved) was also bound to be somewhat painful. Financial straits eventually compelled her to accept the post of assistant almoner at the local hospital. About the same time and for the same reason Dolores took a job as secretary in the welfare department of a large steelworks. Moreover, because Jean was dependent for her happiness upon having Ron in close proximity she felt lonely when he was out night after night on church business.

All this could undoubtedly have been borne and overcome had it not been for the fact that during these four years Jean suffered no less than four miscarriages eventually having a child that was stillborn. Some time after these distressing events there came to stay with the Goldmans a friend who, while appearing quite normal, had a history of mental unbalance. During the period of her visit to the Goldmans she became markedly schizophrenic and the doctor warned them that her tendencies could be equally suicidal or murderous. As it was, this was not fulfilled but Jean had always been on her guard and was compelled to undergo from time to time some very anxious hours during both night and day.

These experiences imposed a nervous and physical strain upon the Goldmans, and especially upon Jean, which went some way to produce the crisis terminating our co-ministry. It was precipitated however not primarily by these domestic hardships but by the trend of events at Masbro' Chapel. In particular by public response to the 'Forward Movement' programme, which aimed to bring more people into our fold by means of visiting them in their homes, and making special provision for the old and the young, among many other initiatives.

In 1952 it was our view that the Forward Movement proposals deserved to focus all the latent energy of the church and certain sections of the programme were not difficult to put into effect, especially those which did not depend for their success on the rank and file of the members. Sadly, support was lacking in certain areas and although we tried hard we were unable to instil much enthusiasm among our members for a comprehensive programme of events.

That year not only saw the failure of the Forward Movement, it also brought a financial crisis. True, during our ministry, income had doubled (though congregations were trebled) and the church had bought not one manse but two. 1950 and 1951 were peak years showing record congregations and offerings – to speak only of measurable assets. But it was a fleeting triumph. Hardly had the summit been reached than the descent began. Instead of people trickling into the church they started to trickle out. Attendances in every department fell off, and an ecclesiastical doctor, feeling the pulse of this Masbro' Chapel fellowship would have diagnosed 'sluggishness' at least.

What was the matter with people? Did the co-ministry have no more than the novelty of a new toy for them, a shining bauble of which they had now tired? How far were we ourselves to blame? Had our work been too superficial, eager to achieve results too quickly, which were incapable of lasting? Should we have sounded a note of deeper challenge and concentrated more intensively upon the need of those inside the church for renewed commitment? On the other hand perhaps people expected too much of us. At the beginning there were those who said within themselves, "Two men together ought to be able to fill this church, and make its rafters ring with the sound of a thousand voices, as in the old days." This may have been the fascinating vision which had filled some people's minds at the start of the co-ministry; they had sat back to watch it happen. When it did not, then we had failed them and disillusion took hold.

One Tuesday, the day of our weekly conference, Ron declared

himself to be "utterly sick" of the ministry, "tired to death" of slaving night and day for the church while seeing it slip back. "Did I go into the ministry on the basis of an inadequate religious experience?" he asked himself, "for motives of power and to feed the super-ego?" He told me how difficult he found it to preach sincerely and to offer public prayer. While still believing in the worth of Christian values, he confessed to having no awareness of the "companionship and love of Christ." The counsellor himself needed counsel, and we discussed these matters together on numerous occasions for a total of many hours.

As the result of the continuing barren course we were both enduring at Masbro' Chapel, Ron's revulsion from the ministry grew stronger as the weeks passed. He felt an increasing urge to withdraw from it and to try something else. With all the personal and public hardships he had experienced this was indeed understandable, though I was grieved at the impasse to which my friend and colleague had come and the fact that I could do little to help him through it except by prayer and, for want of a more precise word, love.

Both Dolores and I could see at length the only way out was a completely new start for the Goldmans, a new field of labour in another place. Ron became desperate, not only to leave Masbro' Chapel and Rotherham, but to withdraw from the pastoral ministry. Throughout an agonising eight months he applied for various jobs (with references supplied by me) including warden of an outward bound school, secretary of a marriage guidance council, city youth leader, and BBC talks producer. He got on the short list for all of these but no further. The church, incidentally, knew nothing of this, or of Ron's personal struggles. Then one day in January 1953 he was offered a job for which he had previously been turned down – lecturer in psychology and social studies at Westhill College. The successful candidate had had a complete nervous and physical breakdown after a few months and would never be able to resume. Ron jumped at the chance, though characteristically persuaded them to put another fifty pounds on the salary before he accepted.

I was now in the same position as ninety-nine point nine per cent of my fellow ministers – alone. The feeling was one of relief after all the tensions of the past year; it was also one of sadness at losing so valuable a friend and colleague; additionally it was one of apprehension as to the future.

Chapter Eleven

A Well-Earned Break

Before I continue with my own personal odyssey I would, for a few paragraphs, like to hand over to my dear late wife, Dolores Grant, who, in 1950, penned a series of observations about life as an American in Britain. Below is an extract from one such missive:

"A new field has opened up. I found myself embarking on that phase of my life, labelled 'The British Worker' – as an employee of SP & T. First as an American citizen, I had to get permission from the United States consulate, fill out forms at the local employment office, the Collector of Internal Revenue, the National Insurance Office, and at SP & T. Then I began.

"Soon it became evident that out of 7,600 employees, 7,599 of them misspelled 'center', 'organize', 'labor', 'program' etc. They even wrote the date backwards putting the day before the month, and some queer abbreviation behind every man's name, an 'esq'. There were other peculiarities...most of which are still waiting to be discovered.

"It all began when I chanced to meet an Englishman in California who, without any of the 'typical British reserve', proposed after a few weeks' acquaintanceship. Six months later we were married in a very 'international wedding', and set out for England. Interspersed with our travels were little lectures from my husband on life in post-war Britain (this was four years ago), British history, British culture – none of which I remembered, except that all the people in England were on the point of starvation and almost freezing to death. I envisaged myself dying at an early age, a martyr to the cause.

"The idea of freezing became a reality, as we arrived in December and I had my first taste of a non-centrally heated house. This brought back memories of the thermostat which was turned down to sixty-five degrees at night and up to seventy or seventy-five degrees during the day. Not even yet have I become accustomed to sleeping in a bedroom without radiators, or taking a bath in an unheated bathroom.

"In these years, I have never ceased to be awed by the lovely green countryside of England, the absolutely exquisite villages, each so distinct from its neighbour, the strikingly diverse scenery crammed within a few square miles, the tiny cars, most of which looked as though they should be nursed until they grew up, the wee railway freight cars, small enough to go in my pocket, English radio minus all those tiresome singing commercials, the delight of listening to a cricket match commentator discussing a man with three legs or one that is silly mid-off, the sedateness of a cricket match audience and the unrepressed vociferousness of the football crowd; and so on.

"I am still agog with the new experiences this country provides for one from another civilization: as an example, eating such things as fried tomatoes and kippers for breakfast; the complicated money system, (even today I can't tell a 2/- and a 2/6 piece apart without reading them); the 100 weight which isn't a 100 weight at all but 120 pounds, the typical British home minus all those appliances which minister to one's comfort. The experience of shopping was particularly difficult as I had to learn to abandon all such words as stores, cookies, cup cakes, corn meal, molasses; even the request for beets never seemed to produce beetroot. I might just as well have asked for it in Apache language. A request for suspenders would not bring forth an item to hold up my husband's pants, but rather his stockings, and when I asked for a wrench from the hardware store, people looked blank. Also I have learned that several harmless slang expressions in the USA have a ghastly meaning in this country, and vice versa. To quote Alastair Cooke: "Naturally, no examples can be given in print (!).""

"I don't suppose I shall ever become accustomed to living in the midst of history – you can easily understand this when you realize our oldest building in San Francisco was erected in 1872, and is preserved as an ancient monument! What a contrast to our parish church or tombs in Westminster dating 900 AD or even going to BC at Stonehenge.

"The phase of a 'British Worker', has just begun, but already the friendliness and helpfulness of people here at SP & T has been most impressive, as well as the patience of the Yorkshireman as I try desperately to understand his lingo (perhaps he's having the same trouble with me). The kindliness of those in the Welfare and Safety Departments who put up with a constant flow of questions, such as "How on earth does one spell this word lorry?" (Truck is so much simpler.) Perhaps in a year or two, I'll make it 7,600 employees who are misspelling all these words, then it will be just my luck to return to the States and have to begin my spelling lessons all over again."

In 1954 Dolores and I had now been in England for five years. For someone who had never been east of Chicago before and who had come straight from the gleaming beauty and fascination of San Francisco to the muck heaps of Rotherham my wife had settled down wonderfully well. There had never been any doubt about her ability to cope with English life even though it was not until years after our arrival that she discovered that a 'dry closet' is a chemical lavatory and not a damp-proof wardrobe, and that domestic gas has to be manufactured from coal instead of coming from subterranean deposits beneath the soil of Texas. It could not be said that Dolores was ever really homesick, but there was a natural desire after five years abroad, to see her parents, grandparents, four brothers and innumerable friends again. As for me, I yearned to renew my acquaintance with a country in which there were so many people for whom I had come to have an affectionate regard.

In 1951 Dolores had secured secretarial work with a local firm to supplement my meagre salary (she had to borrow a decent pair of shoes in which to go for the interview). As the result of Ron's departure however, the church had been able to give me in 1951 the substantial rise of £4 a week, so that my salary was now £11. Owing to our simple way of living we were able to make ends meet on this. Therefore all that Dolores earned was saved and an American trip began to come within our economic reach. We decided to try to go for six months if the church would grant me absence of leave. A talk with Frank Wragg and Charles Chislett convinced me they would, and at the next church meeting we both withdrew while the affair was discussed. Upon re-entry to the lecture hall we were astonished to be greeted by a pronged burst of applause. Frank Wragg explained that the church had gladly and unanimously given me permission to be absent for six months and laid the seal of its blessing upon our plan. The church had also, he said, decided to pay me half salary for the time I was away (the only dissentient from this, I discovered later, was Mrs Twigg who thought I should be on full salary for the period of absence).

This very generous offer I immediately declined both on the ground that during these six months I should not in fact be doing any work for the chapel and also that an acceptance of the money would be unfair to those who made real monetary sacrifices for the church. Besides, the salary of a temporary minister would have to be paid. As a compromise I agreed that the church should paint the hallway and staircase of the manse. We ourselves were normally responsible for all the interior decorations to the ten-roomed house.

Private reactions to our proposed trip differed widely. Mrs Twigg was so delighted by this respite from us that she gave Dolores £20 with which to buy clothes – knowing that for a long time the Minister's wife could not afford to be as well dressed as most other women in the congregation.

Others less kindly and sensitive opined, "You might as well say goodbye to him; once she gets him over there there'll be no coming back." From every point of view this was a gross misreading of Dolores' attitude. One deacon expressed his fear to me that, "All the good work of the last five years will be lost. You may have to start all over again," he said. I replied that it would be a test as to whether a church can stand on its own feet and not lean for support on a particular personality. "In any case," I told him, "a good man will be brought in for this period."

That proved to be easier to say than to do. The matter was left to me and for several months I scoured the denomination without success. My mind was made up that if I could find no one to take full charge of Masbro' I would cancel the whole project. At last, in desperation I advertised in the denominational newspaper. There were fourteen replies. One or two were from retired men well over seventy years of age. Others came from those who, as the result of personal defalcations, had been blacklisted by every major denomination. Some of these sent voluminous testimonials which represented them as gems of pure genius, unblemished saintliness, and super-human vigour. There were even a couple of men so desperate to move from their present charges that they begged to be allowed to come, knowing it was for only six months. Finally, three possibilities were sorted out, none of whom were very highly recommended by the denominational authorities. One of these, a sixty-four year old retired minister and now a part-time welfare officer at a factory, came up to Rotherham so that we could engage in a mutual appraisal. The result was that he agreed to come four days a week including Sunday at a salary of £8.

It was now possible to make definite arrangements for the trip. There were two reasons why we were going to have to be self-supporting for those six months. One was that the British government at that time forbade American-bound travellers to take with them more than £35 each, in sterling. The other was that in any case we would not have had the resources to keep us going for very long. In two respects at least fortune was smiling on us. From coast to coast relatives and friends waited, in fact had been waiting ever since our departure five years before, to welcome us with accommodation and sustenance. There also existed churches and other organizations within my acquaintance which could be prevailed upon to engage my services, professional or otherwise. Eventually I gave lectures at Boston University, carried out a short summer ministry at a church in Berkeley, California, spoke at several Rotary clubs and preached in a dozen different churches. Thanks to the wonderful hospitality of our friends, during the whole six months we had to stay in hotels only in Cheyenne, Wyoming; El Paso, Texas, and New Orleans. The British government's allocation to us of £35 each was gone within the first few weeks, and although at no time were our wallets bulging with dollars, the mercies of the good Lord provided us with enough, in fact with more than enough, for after travelling 15,000 miles we arrived home with tuppence.

The day prior to our embarkation at Hull was a Sunday and my evening sermon dealt with Jacob's ignominious flight from the clutches of Laban. This story contains the famous and misunderstood injunction 'Let the Lord watch between thee and me when we are absent one from another'. Though the congregation was led to perceive a faint parallel between Jacob's situation and mine, I did not, like him, move off from Godstone Road with five hundred cows and two wives seated upon camels. In fact, having learned by wretched experience to travel light, I took only two suitcases and one wife. Friends drove us by Alfa-Romeo to board our ship, the 7,000 ton Consuelo.

In spite of the fact that five years before Dolores and I had enjoyed travelling on the world's largest liner, with its sophisticated social life and hotel-like amenities, we much preferred the simpler, more intimate type of shipboard life to be found in smaller vessels, cargo carriers especially. That is why we chose the Consuelo, carrying pitch, sewage pipes and cars to Canada. In addition to ourselves, four other passengers boarded for the voyage, all immigrants – a young Scottish fisherman with wife and baby, and an avidly-Bible-reading builder bound for Calgary. The only trouble with these ships is that their date and time of departure is apt to fluctuate with cargo requirements. We were therefore in almost semi-panic when soon after having given us a provisional sailing date seventeen days ahead, the company rang up to say that the ship would after all be departing in three days time – and this was a Sunday! In the circumstances we were grateful for the offer of some friends to drive us to our ship. How delightful it was to find awaiting us in the cabin a splendid bouquet of flowers and half a dozen *bon voyage* telegrams from Masbro' Chapel. It took nearly a week to convince the captain we were not a honeymoon couple.

After lunch a solitary racehorse was embarked by crane and lowered into the recesses of number three hold. For the twelve day voyage it stood upright in its narrow stall and was visited regularly by our fellow passengers who discovered that the equine digestive system apparently retains a more beautiful tranquillity than its counterpart when subject to the motion of the sea. When we saw this animal coming aboard we had visions of us all taking turns riding it around the deck every morning for exercise, after the style of the naval cavalry. But when I mentioned it to the captain he seemed to think it not a very good idea. At 4.30pm aided by nosing and hooting tugs, Consuelo slid out into the bleak and dirty waters of the Humber.

Next morning the coast of Scotland was visible six miles to port and soon the spires of Aberdeen – the Granite City – loomed through distant haze. During the next twenty-four hours, while Consuelo discharged her cargo of flour, we roamed the city streets buying last minute gifts for friends. In Rotherham someone had given us a dozen miniature models of the Coronation coach complete with horses, riders and the Queen and Duke inside. Our Anglophile friends could not wish for presents more unmistakeably English. In the evening when we were desirous of seeing a film, I suggested that *The Monster from 20,000 Fathoms* might appeal to our sense of humour, but Dolores thought it was a somewhat inappropriate prelude to the hazards of a transatlantic voyage midwinter. So we went instead to the Tivoli Music Hall where the Scottish Puritanism of the management and the Irish Catholic morality of the artists combined to prove that a show can be hilariously comic without stooping to indecency.

Almost from the start our captain was a puzzle to us. His face had been carved into an elaborate system of crags and gulleys by half a lifetime of Atlantic weather. They puckered up into creases when he laughed which was often. He could afford to laugh and be at ease, for here he was a man, we sensed, who knew his job from top to bottom. Yet it wasn't long before we began to have doubts about our captain, doubts of a kind which set us thinking about Heaven and our next of kin. For example, approaching Pentland Firth he began warning us of difficulties involved in negotiating these narrows, especially in the dark. "No more than two miles wide," he said, "and bristling with rocks; doubt if we shall make it." We each drew a mental picture of Consuelo charging up the main street of John O'Groats, splitting the town in half and make it necessary to go through customs all over again.

And then there was the time when winches got up steam and sounded off like volcanoes on the verge of eruption. It resulted in the good captain rushing downstairs from his room to the lounge where we were peacefully seated and shouting wildly at nobody in particular that the ship was blowing up. This performance, which we rewarded with a beam, convinced us that life on a small freighter is infinitely more entertaining than on some monster vessel like the Queen Elizabeth where one never saw the captain.

Nevertheless we began to wonder what sort of maniac this was to whom our lives were entrusted. One day after lunch, I cornered the chief engineer and asked him if Captain Goodman had ever lost any passengers and if so, how? His only reply was to look shifty and turn silently away. That settled it. The five of us decided we would deliberately test the captain to see how much he really knew about navigation. At dinner I was deputed to ask a series of bold questions, the first of which was, "Where are we now, Captain?" and within earshot of all his officers who sat at the next table, he replied, "I haven't the slightest idea." At this point the Scottish fisherman's wife choked on her soup and the silent, Bible-studying builder lifted his eyes to the sky. Determined to develop the probe, I said, "Would it be possible for the wind during the night to have turned us completely around without anybody knowing so that we are now on our way back to England?"

"We shall know," he replied, "when the Canadian radio stations start getting fainter again." The steward then asked me if I would care for a portion of Sir Watkin pudding. I said I might as well, and the rest of the meal was spent in silent meditation.

After only a few hundred miles out from Aberdeen, I had the misfortune to be absent from the captain's table for a few days, owing to a combination of human foolishness and meteorological conditions. In a storm which set the ship on its beam ends I managed one day at breakfast – a glass of tomato juice, porridge, curried lamb and rice, and I got half way though bacon and egg before abdominal seethings propelled me from the table. Thereafter I lay in bed and ate nothing for three days, except a few chicken sandwiches and a bottle of ginger ale. In the midst of my misery, Dolores came down, put her hand sympathetically on my shoulder and murmured, "Cheer up, only another 2,400 miles to go."

To try and keep my mind off the sickness, I repeated the Latin mnemonic for remembering types of syllogisms – Barbara, Celarent, Darii, ferioque prioris...and also the little waves of Breffny ('the little waves of Breffny have drenched my heart in spray, and the little waves of Breffny go stumbling through my soul'). Between bouts of sleep and restless tossing I eventually got through the *Seven Pillars of Wisdom*.

At length both the weather and I came back to normal and it was once more possible to wade through enormous menus without fear of stomachial convolutions. Life settled down to a sumptuous routine.

Just when everyone began to recover enough for the enjoyment of such a carefree life, up the Bay of Fundy we came and docked at St John, New Brunswick on a bright, clear, cold-hard morning. As we drove to see American immigration authorities, the horse feeding chief officer called after us, "If they ask you what colour the ship's funnel is, say blue." (Senator Joe McCarthy was at the height of his notoriety in

1954.) The solitary immigration official asked us only one question – "Are you a Communist?" He did not put the question to Dolores as she was travelling on an American passport. Did he believe that by such refine sleuthing he was going to be able to smell me out if I was indeed an enemy of the state? Were immigration officials compelled by law to ask such questions? Or did they think it up for themselves?

By sitting on an overnight train we were able to be in Augusta, Maine at 4am on Sunday morning. Though the winter snows were still about and we were tired and hungry, we walked about almost with a feeling of intoxication engendered by the thrill of having American soil under our feet again after an absence of five and a half years. There were three restaurants open serving breakfast, and a drug store – this at 4.30am on a Sunday morning. Imagine that for a town of only 20,000 people! I nearly burst with excitement; such a thing would not be possible even in London, and as for Rotherham (four times the size of Augusta) there was not a single café or restaurant open at any hours on a Sunday.

After coffee and bacon we wandered the streets and gaped about us like men newly landed on a strange planet, and at 11am tried to be anonymous in a large crowd at the Congregational church. But it was no use. As strangers we were spotted immediately, and when worship finished information was drawn from us that we were not only fleeting visitors to Maine, but wanderers returning to civilization after five years in the Great Beyond. Because of this, people were eager to open their hearts and homes for our pleasure. We had planned to continue on down to Boston that day but gladly accepted an invitation to dinner one family gave us. They were our friends within the hour, though we never saw them again. Occasionally correspondence still passes between us – and stamps for our respective albums. Thus we were re-introduced at the start of our tour to that spontaneous hospitality and immediate friendship which must surely be unsurpassed in the world. It made our progress across the States delightful.

Engagements took me through Connecticut, New York,

Pennsylvania, Delaware, Michigan, and Illinois. At Hinsdale I was able to bring greetings and gratitude from Masbro' Chapel to the church whose members had made the co-ministry possible by their gift of one salary for two years. After brief visits in Wisconsin we spent some weeks with Dolores' parents and grandparents in Iowa before travelling west again by bus. British long distance buses were about as comfortable as ox carts compared with the smooth-riding luxury of American coaches. And the people one met were not quite so richly varied either. Quiet conformity to the 'accepted behaviour pattern' was obviously an appealing mode of conduct to the man who sat behind us in the bus between Laramie and Fort Rawlings. I had not noticed him before but when getting back on after lunch I was just about to sit down when he suddenly gripped me by the arms. This fellow was well-built, with a face the colour of dough, bullet-headed, glazed eyes and flattened nose.

Startled by having my arms pinioned, I said, "Do you wish to pass?" "No," he replied. "Then allow me to sit down," I insisted. He did. After a few minutes he spoke to me again, "I want to examine your baggage. I'm from the San Francisco police." I said, "Let me see your authorization." At that he was silent, but bent over Dolores from the seat behind and showed her a piece of paper on which was written the words, 'I could not show it to him'. She ignored him. However, he still insisted upon searching my baggage but I was adamant in refusing, "All right then," he declared, "I'll search somebody else's." He went along the bus, got down the case of a man who was sleeping, looked inside, put it back and said, "Perfectly innocent, perfectly innocent."

I tried to settle down with a book, but this creature behind me began to lean forward and jab me in the ribs. The jabbing was accompanied by derogatory remarks in which I was referred to as 'poor old Joe'. Turning round at last I snorted at him, giving vent to a foolish inflammatory remark – "Why don't you go and jab someone else for a change?" In order not to get mixed up in these strange goings on all the other folk in the bus pretended to be asleep, but upon hearing this they opened their eyes in alarm. But there was no need; the man was apparently interested only in me. Suddenly I was conscious of an outstretched hand poised above my head and before I could turn round it had seized a fist full of hair which was used as a handle to shake my whole body from side to side. Before I could recover properly from this the hand had seized Dolores's head and she too was shaken from side to side. At this I leapt from my seat and was all for throwing the lout out of the window, but Dolores restrained me saying, "Keep him quiet, pacify him, smile amiably." In the circumstances I found this extremely difficult to do, but sat down again. Then the man got up, bent forward and gave Dolores a smacking great kiss. That settled it; in spite of the uninhabited country through which we were passing, I would ask the driver to put him off. But before I did this, Dolores tried to get his destination and asked, "Where are you going?" He replied, "To church, to marry your sister." By this time we were running into Fort Rawlings and there the 'Man from Laramie' got off. When I told the driver what had happened he said "If I'd known about that guy, I'd have dumped him on the road, no matter where it was."

San Francisco drew us more magnetically to itself than any other city in America. Apart from its dazzling situation, semi-oriental flavour, and cultural excitements, this city brought back to us the most tender of personal memories. Here we had spent our courting days, here we were married at the Fellowship Church of All Peoples where Dolores was secretary, and here we lived in 1948 until our departure for England. During these few weeks of my short ministry in Berkeley delicious hours were spent renewing friendships, re-visiting favourite restaurants, and reviving romantic emotions at nostalgically remembered venues.

At length, pushing south, we stayed for a few days with an old lady in Hollywood previously acquainted with us; a mutual friend had been the means of our receiving an invitation. Two facts at least made her interesting; she was reputed to be worth $15 million and she had the most remarkable notions about diet. Upon arrival we were given separate bedrooms and bathrooms. The latter were tiled throughout and were each about as large as the four rooms of a Masbro' terrace house knocked into one. Mrs S was an extremely gracious woman but almost at once started talking to us about food. She had made some discoveries; one of them was tiger's milk. This consisted of a glass of milk into which were heaped a spoonful each of brewer's yeast, blackstrap molasses, soya flour and powdered liver. It was a horrible mixture but we had to drink the stuff down each day and were assured that what spinach does for Popeye, tiger's milk would do for us. The effect was certainly good – once we had it in pomegranate juice – and from then on Dolores and I took a weakened form of the health-giving potion. (I recommended it to Ministers in Fraternals in a talk entitled 'How to be healthy though a parson'.) Every night upon going to bed Mrs S also gave us a nightcap sandwich. This was a three-inch square of liver sausage between equal size pieces of cheese. "You'll be rippling with energy, pulsating with life," she said. Certainly the lady herself was no mean advertisement for the diet and at seventy-six looked twenty years younger.

Not all rich people are generous with their money, but Mrs S was one of the few. Horrified we were planning to travel from Los Angeles to New Orleans by so plebeian means as a bus ("You'll be terribly tired.") she gave us the money to go by train. It was a substantial sum, for the distance was nearly two thousand miles. The 'Sunset Limited', took us through Arizona, Texas to El Paso. There I bought a ten-gallon hat which eventually had to be worn both in France and England on the way home owing to the impossibility of packing it. On the streets of these two countries children walked backwards two or three feet in front of us so that they could get a better look.

The eighteen-day sunshine voyage from New Orleans to Le Havre in an American freighter purged away the memory we still had of the Atlantic in winter. Hugging the American coast to give us an extra eighty mile a day push provided by the Gulf Stream, our route home described a parabola across smooth sunlit seas. With three other passengers and 4,000 tons of sulphur the James Lykes was a similar type of vessel to the Consuelo, but the respective ship's companies differed enormously and somehow typified divergences between British and American character.

On the Consuelo discipline was rigid and uniforms *de rigeur*. The captain was called 'Sir' when addressed and even on so small a ship the officers sat in strict seniority for their meals, being immaculate in white shirts, black ties and gold-braided uniform. Tables were set in the best spotless tradition of London hotels, and if the captain found a few grains adhering to the sugar spoon, the steward would be ordered to bring a clean one at once.

In the American ship on the other hand, it was impossible to distinguish between the captain and say, the third engineer. All the officers appeared to be wearing their old clothes – a baggy pair of flannels and a silk shirt. They all sat where they liked for meals and addressed the captain as 'Tom'.

Moreover, though we sensed the kitchen on the Consuelo was something of a holy preserve and would not have dared enter it, the American ship's captain made it clear that we could go into the kitchen and make coffee whenever we wished. The only stipulation was that we should fill up the pot again. We enjoyed the breezy informality of life aboard Jams Lykes but at the same time appreciated the smartness and precision of British Merchant Marines.

Crossing over from Le Havre to Southampton by British Railways' steamer, we finally arrived in Rotherham grateful for rich experiences, eager to see all our friends again, but also apprehensive as to what the future held for us at Masbro' Chapel. With dry mouth and tightened-up throat I was dismayed to find myself in the grip of fear as our taxi drove us toward Godstone Road and the severe realities of ministerial life.

The church hailed our return with obvious pleasure. In addition to the young people who staged a special evening for us, at which I was persuaded to wear my newly-acquired authentic cowboy outfit, the whole body of members put on a supper to mark our home-coming. The tables were decorated with British and American flags and speeches of welcome were given which betrayed the church's relief that we had come home at all! Hope was expressed that we should be at Masbro' for a "long time". But inevitably there were one or two folk, mostly outside the church, who whispered we had only come back to clear our affairs before returning to the States.

Chapter Twelve

The Founding of Herringthorpe

Far from scarpering back to the United States at the first opportunity, there was still much work to be done in Rotherham, and in particular in the neighbouring district of Herringthorpe, where a long-promised Free Church was waiting to be built. The land had been purchased in 1933, but behind the wooden board which said 'Site of Congregational Church' rows of cabbages were growing, as they had done for years. A farmer rented the ground for a small annual payment until such time as a church should be built.

And when would that be? For nearly twenty years people riding up and down on the trolley buses had seen the notice; it had become a fixture. If they had ever speculated as to when the church was going to be built, by 1954 they had probably stopped and finally put it down as one of those events whose date – like that of the Last Judgement – is unknowable to finite minds, and far enough away to deter most people from thinking about it. But there were folk thinking about it and who were determined that a new Congregational church should rise on the site – before the Day of Judgement if possible. Some of the Congregationalists whose foresight and vision had led to the purchase of the ground in 1933 were now dead, but others still lived and a new generation had grown up who rose to the challenge of that cabbage field.

In 1954, however, they still had a long way to go. The Sunday school, commenced eighteen months before at the local primary school, had grown slowly until attendance topped the fifty mark. The Methodists, with a head start of ten years, had creamed off most of the children from families with Free Church leanings. Some of our older scholars were already in their teens and having had the milk, were ready for the meat of the Gospel. The point had been reached where the formation of a church was a logical and imperative necessity; it could be delayed no longer.

Several ardent spirits clamoured for a service to be held at the same time on Sunday mornings as the Sunday school. Their intuition told them that, once started, it would gather a larger morning congregation than Masbro' and the Roman Catholic church put together. Naturally, though I was precluded by my Masbro' duties from having any official part in the Sunday school, I joined in conversations about these matters. Clearly, it seemed to me that unless a church could be formed now and services held each week, cabbages would probably grow for ever on our precious site and the work of the Sunday school lead to nothing.

It must be done, but how? When all those interested parties met informally to lay plans, the biggest problem of all was to see where preachers were coming from to conduct weekly worship. In Rotherham there were only two ministers and these were fully engaged at their own churches on Sunday. True, a dozen lay preachers supplemented the ministerial strength but in addition to the job of conducting Sunday evening services at small outlying chapels they were generally men who carried a heavy work load at their own churches. One deacon presided over the Masbro' Chapel Sunday school every Sunday afternoon for example, and often a village congregation in the evening. As the owner of a business his time for thinking, reading and relaxing with his family, was nearly squeezed out of the programme. Moreover, we knew him to be under some gentle fire from his wife owing to the fact that his Sunday duties prevented them from having weekend enjoyment at their caravan on the coast. Other lay preachers had their own peculiar difficulties.

Suddenly an idea came to me as though the strong beam of a headlamp had been switched on to make it visible in the darkness. Why not ask Masbro' Chapel to release me from the morning service so that I could give Herringthorpe a good start with theirs? I did not expect them to let me go every Sunday, but they might agree to two a month, and on those occasions the service at Masbro' would be given over entirely to the children – there were usually forty of them to about a dozen or twenty adults. Those who were not trained lay preachers could preside at such a service. Then, of course, if lay preachers were able to fill in the intervening Sundays by rota the extra burden would not fall very heavily on any of them.

Everybody thought the scheme a good one, including Masbro' Chapel deacons. A church meeting was called after service one Sunday night to decide about it. My sermon had dealt with the 'Creative Power of Imagination' without actually mentioning the matter to be discussed. But it had its effect. The members' imagination was stirred by the prospect at Herringthorpe and when a resolution was being considered, one leading light in the Arrow Club, jumped up and said, "How dare we not vote for it after hearing tonight's sermon?" The vote was unanimous, though some were not happy about having Masbro's own morning service 'downgraded' as they called it. That could not be helped. Notwithstanding the fact that Masbro' was going to lose part of its minister's time and energy by this arrangement, a few words of praise and encouragement to the venture were coupled with the resolution. This was Masbro' Chapel at its best; here was the kind of inspired Christian magnanimity and initiative that in 200 years had launched more that a dozen churches and given the chapel a reputation for 'rising to the big occasion'. Proof was here that in extreme age the old lady was not completely 'cribbed, cabined and confined'.

The leap of faith was not unjustified. Within a few weeks a congregation of about forty adults was gathered as well as the children who dispersed to their classes about halfway through morning worship. The prophet was right who suggested that congregations would exceed those at Masbro'. Indeed, I did not know of any Free Church in Rotherham which could muster more than forty worshippers on a Sunday morning.

The circular high-domed school hall in which we met, with its long blackboard, noisy wooden floors, tubular chairs and bad acoustics was not an ideal place for worship, but I always felt a sense of excitement and worthwhileness in preaching to that newly-formed congregation. It seemed that they were alert and listening with eager attention. This was probably true of Masbro's morning congregation too, though I often did not feel it, especially as the dozen or twenty people were scattered about in seats meant for 1,200. The ride from my home to Masbro' was nearly all downhill and to Herringthorpe it was uphill, but in spite of this, on those mornings when I had to ride to Herringthorpe I stuffed my gown and hood into the bicycle saddle bag with a fresher enthusiasm, and in running the machine out onto the roadway felt stimulated by the knowledge that my mission on these particular mornings was part of a significantly creative act.

Who were these worshippers at Herringthorpe? Two were men without previous church connections. One of them, a bank clerk, was appointed treasurer of the new church and eventually became a deacon. All the others had had church affiliations at some period, but which for various reasons had been allowed to lapse. Now, appropriately in a new church, they were giving themselves a new start. Not all had so serious a motive as this – they came out of curiosity. Most were brought by friends. There was one important exception to this, a middle-aged man with his wife and five-year-old boy. They turned up at Masbro' one Sunday morning and caused great consternation merely by being there. Strangers were so rarely seen at any service that the utmost curiosity was aroused when they did come. At the close of worship the man said something to me that no one had ever said before. "My wife and I are looking for a church where we feel we can settle," he began. "Actually we are Baptists from Derby and though we have lived in Rotherham a few years we have never attended a church here, but now the youngster is growing up we feel that it is time to form a proper connection with one again." How exhilarating it was to hear, for the first time, someone speak like this.

"Where do you live?" I asked. He mentioned a road two miles away from Masbro', but only a few minutes walk from Herringthorpe. "We should like to have you here at Masbro' Chapel," I told him, "but we have just started a new church almost on your doorstep – perhaps you would enjoy going there one Sunday." He said they would – and they did. It seems to be just the right sort of place for a youngish couple with children, and they settled happily in the church. He proved himself to be a gift from God which came just at the right time. His arrival coincided with Herringthorpe's decision to build and the necessity for having someone of driving force in the church with a technical knowledge of building plans who could steer us through all the complications involved was Heaven-sent. This was exactly his line of country and he even had the advantage of having worked on building projects with the architect we eventually chose. When the whole building plan began to be created he rolled up his sleeves, immersed himself in the work and was soon made chairman of the building committee.

But this is running ahead. By far the largest single group – though still a minority in the new church, especially after May 1955 – were members of the old Rotherham Congregational church. "They are malcontents and trouble-makers," I was told about a few of them. They were painted jet-black by others who had formerly attended the old church. The people who thus complained to me I immediately invited to the Herringthorpe services, hoping they would join up with the new church. But it was no good. "If so-and-so are there," they declared, "you'll not get me in it, even if it is the last church on earth." Some of those, who said this never did come, others buried the hatchet and were received into membership. I was always on the alert for trouble, but a new spirit seemed to prevail amongst former enemies and I did not find evidence of any unrest, except on one occasion later on.

Though services were held regularly from the first Sunday of January 1955, it was not until a few months later that members 'covenanted together' thus forming themselves formally into a church and becoming affiliated to the Congregational Union of England and Wales. Work and witness were severely restricted by the fact that the school premises could not be hired to us except for Sunday mornings, and thus mid-week activities were impossible.

The infant church was, of course, very much under Masbro' Chapel's wing and often listened dutifully to mother's whispered advice. This was given through an interchange of officials who attended every meeting of the church and its committees. Moreover, within a few months I suddenly realised that I was now – in practice if not in theory – minister of the new church. The situation was accepted tacitly both at Herringthorpe and Masbro', without it being mentioned on either side. I found myself presiding at every Herringthorpe church meeting, most committees – held in members' homes – visiting the sick and aged, burying the dead, christening the newborn, and negotiating in all kinds of affairs on behalf of this small but growing flock.

From the start, everyone was eager to build, yet no one could see how it was going to be done. A simple box-like building to hold 200 plus a small room with a seating capacity of thirty would cost £10,000, and the church's financial resources were almost nil; Masbro' Chapel held £600 in trust against the day when the building should be started. This had been given years before by certain visionaries who were now dead. We could not expect much help from the denomination; for a new church building throughout the whole country only £3,000 was available in central funds. Towards the end of 1955, however, our hopes rose. The old Rotherham Congregational church was sold to the town by compulsory purchase order for £5,000, and after mortgages of £1,050 were deducted, the balance was handed over to Herringthorpe for its building fund. What a lift for our morale this was! Already we could see the cabbages going and the bricks coming.

Over a period of several years our Appeals Committee devised all kinds of ways to raise money. The inevitable jumble sales were held at a hired hall in town. Paper bricks were sold at six pence each; scholars collected money on subscription cards at one penny each; members took home cardboard boxes made in the shape of a three penny piece and eventually filled them with £2 of that coin. Whist and beetle drives, bring-and-buy sales, film shows and garden parties nudged up the total. But with all these devices, the thousands more we needed were still out of reach – until the northern headquarters of the denomination came to our aid. Years before, a couple of redundant churches in pit villages not far away had been closed and sold, the £2,000 proceeds 'frozen' in a special account and earmarked for future church development in the area. We were now to have the money. My position as district secretary, which took me to meetings at the northern headquarters, enabled me to plead in person on behalf of Herringthorpe. To the appropriate committees I said, "This young church is one of the most promising in the north. When most churches are on the decline this one is on the way up. Remember the new churches in this district which after ten years or more have less than twenty members and now tremble on the verge of extinction, and then look at Herringthorpe which has forty active members, mostly younger people who are keen and able to work..."

I did not have to plead – they knew the situation well enough, and as a result £600 was scraped up from somewhere. Representations on our behalf were now made in London, where they did not know the situation. A strong case was put forward and we were promised £800 from two different funds. And in addition to all this, Masbro' herself promised to donate £300 a year for the next few years.

The jubilation which marked this progress brought simultaneous frustration in other ways. Our architect was well chosen. As a keen member of a Congregational church in a nearby city, his work for us was going to be more than the fulfilment of a professional engagement; it would be the expression of religious faith. Moreover, he had already built half a dozen churches since the war and these had won him an award from the bishop of the diocese for the best designed building.

"Can you create for us something strikingly modern, yet dignified?" we asked him, "nothing neo-Gothic, nor yet a no-period nondescript piece. What we want is something that is obviously a church, but so arresting in appearance that people will stop their cars to see it as they come down the Wickersley Road. Can you do anything like that?"

"Yes, I think so," the tall, gentle and smiling architect said.

"And can you do it for no more than £10,000?"

Now he was only tall and gentle. "Well," he hesitated, "I'll try." And gradually the smile broke out again.

Several weeks later when the plans came through, and many weeks after that when the quantity surveyor produced his estimate, we were all shaken rigid. As drawn, the building was going to cost nearly £18,000. Such a sum was nearly double the amount we possessed and far more than could ever be raised in the foreseeable future. Obviously, a miscalculation had been made, and the plans were sent back. Work had to start all over again and for various reasons this meant a delay of nine months before new ones were ready.

In the meantime, the church continued to expand slowly. I found evidence to suggest that quite a number of interested people were postponing their association with the church until a building was actually erected. "When are you going to get that new church up?" they would ask me. "When that day comes you will see us in the congregation." My reply was always, "It would be up much sooner if you all came and helped us now." Most of these people were afraid that if they came in before sufficient money was raised we should drop on them for more than they were prepared to give. One of the oddest excuses for avoiding full commitment was given by the school caretaker at Herringthorpe. He would not become a member, he said, until it was clear to him that everybody else was in earnest!

Sometimes I used to wonder myself about this. There were plenty of good workers, proportionately more than at Masbro', but they had their occasional lapses. For example, when over sixty people were asked to indicate on a returnable form which of six different kinds of gifts they would be prepared to donate to a bring-and-buy sale only four of the forms were returned and arrangements were completely jeopardised by this failure. Yes, life could be very difficult at times even at Herringthorpe where the mood was so vitally different from that at Masbro'. While the caretaker waited to see if other people were in earnest, he gradually became much less than earnest himself. For some time he was chairman of the social committee whose task it was to organise money-raising functions. One night the management committee of the church was all set to hear an eagerly awaited report from him on proposed future activities, and at that meeting it was to be the chief business for discussion. But he did not turn up. Thinking that something serious must have happened, I called in to see him on the way home. He was sitting happily in front of the fire.

"Did you forget the meeting?" I asked.

"Oh no," he replied. "I was on my way up but I met someone I knew and he kept me talking, and then it was a bit too late to come."

I found it difficult at that moment to keep myself under control. In the end, he and his pleasant, though much-dominated, wife faded from the scene – two of the very few to do so who had once put their hands to the plough.

One of the worst bits of trouble I had to deal with at Herringthorpe involved a flare-up of old animosities breaking out in the new church and I was determined to extinguish it. Upon my arriving home late one night a deputation of three Herringthorpe women were waiting to see me. They were members of the social committee of which the caretaker was chairman, and they wished to accuse the bazaar committee of usurping their prerogative in arranging a Pea and Pie Supper without prior consultation. They wanted me to restrain the high-handed chairman of that committee who was too truculent for them to deal with!

It was clear, however, that the people they had really got their knife into were certain members of that committee who had held opposing views when they had all been members at the old church.

"Mrs R openly sniggers at my husband," one of them complained. "She'd like to get him out of the church if she could. In fact she makes insulting remarks to everybody and cuts them dead it they don't like it."

"But she doesn't do it to me and Mr J," I retorted.

"No, of course not," went on Mrs H, "she's too clever to fall into the trap of doing it to important people."

"You really hate this woman don't you?" I said.

She replied with venom, "I would not degrade myself to do it."

"That means that you hate her more than I thought."

After a backwards-and-forwards argument I said, "If you feel these people need to be changed – and we could all do with a bit of that – it can only be done by praying for them, and you can't both pray for them and hate them at the same time. If you think they have warped personalities, remember they aren't wholly responsible for that and they require to be approached with understanding. There are only two alternatives – let it break you down or master it, to become like them, hateful and insulting, or to have prayerful goodwill, tolerance and a modicum of humour. You must choose between these two approaches. The first will lead to division and disaster, the second to unity of purpose through the possibility of the offender being changed and perhaps you will feel that you need to be changed too. This is a test of your faith and it may be very difficult for you, but no one has ever pretended that the Christian life isn't."

Their flood of words dried up eventually and after a cup of coffee they went – a good deal more humble than when they came in. Fortunately there was never any more trouble of that kind. Not long after, someone said to me, "They'd all be squabbling like a lot of cats if you weren't here." But, in spite of the above incident, I could not believe it.

During this interim period when we were waiting for the new plans and for some time before that, the appeals committee had launched two money-raising schemes which it was hoped would bring in many hundreds of pounds. But both were failures.

The first was an appeal for donations from nearly 100 business concerns in the district. An attractively printed brochure went out with a personal letter to the head of each firm. This bore my signature and that of our 'chief man' in Herringthorpe. He was certainly the wealthiest, and owned a twenty-roomed mansion out in the country originally built 400 years ago as a shooting lodge for the Duke of Norfolk and was now a beautifully modern home, sumptuously furnished. He not only possessed private means, but was one of the foremost businessmen in the district, being commercial director of a large boiler-making firm that bore his name. Therefore he knew, either personally or by repute, the heads of most of the companies whom we approached. Both of us surmised that a letter over his signature would at least guarantee to save it from the waste-paper basket. But we were mistaken. From about seventy of the appeals sent out no reply was ever received, even after a follow-up note two or three months later. About ten others wrote and excused themselves on various grounds. ("Our firm does not do that sort of thing." "We have already expended our charity quota for the year.") The remainder sent mostly small amounts ranging from one guinea to ten guineas. The two largest gifts were £50 from the director of a firm having connections with Herringthorpe and £100 from a gigantic industrial combine whose profits for the year were £18 million. Some of their works were in Rotherham and two or three of their employees belonged to Herringthorpe church. The donation was given on the grounds that one or two more of them might donate as well. Not long afterwards the small and unimposing cathedral in our diocese appealed for funds to extend its medieval building. This same firm donated £50,000 and when the tower of our Rotherham parish church needed repairing nearly every business concern in the town rushed to make its contribution.

This is no complaint but another illustration of the fact that the *established* church has a 'pull' with the public in securing funds which cannot be matched by other churches. The smaller denominations are regarded as representing 'sectarian religion' which, whatever else it may mean, is assumed to be something inferior to the real thing.

The other money-raising project sponsored by the appeals committee was even more of a fiasco – a house-to-house collection. It was prepared with great care, visitors were briefed, special literature was printed and delivered beforehand, and prayer was offered for Divine help. "This is going to be your church," householders were told, "for you and your children. What will you give to help it get built?" Most of them would give nothing because they could not care less whether a church replaced cabbages or not. They had no interest in any church, nor ever attended worship. On those rare occasions when a baby needed christening or a daughter marrying or a mother-in-law burying, there was an Anglican church somewhere nearby that would do it – indeed, had to do it by law. That was the church. Who are these Congregationalists anyway?

Such was the attitude one could sense behind the blank faces of those who said, "Sorry, we are Church of England." If all these protesters had been at matins or evensong on Sunday, no church could have squeezed them in! Of course there were a few genuine ones, and a few who actively supported other churches, but those professing even a vague interest in the possibility of a Congregational church were almost non-existent. A retired policeman and his wife said they would like to come to an evening service and were willing to give a covenanted subscription. The few others who contributed gave only paltry sums and from one road of eighty houses only 17/6d was collected. The result of this visitation was a big shock to us all, not so much because of the pittance it brought in, but because of the widespread lack of interest it reflected in the church, and more particularly Herringthorpe Congregational church.

Our new plans came through in the summer of 1957. Even though members of the building committee and me had been working in close collaboration with the architect, the plans could be brought no lower without violating basic necessities. They provided for a dual purpose building of strikingly unusual design, capable of seating 180 in comfort, a small minister's vestry, kitchen, toilets and a meeting room for about thirty people. The total cost was £12,000, excluding furnishings. We counted our money up, found we had £11,000 and gave our much-relieved architect the green light to go ahead, relying on faith to bring the rest of the money in.

Eventually the funds were raised and the cutting of the first sod took place on 22 February 1958. The church was completed on time. However there was a small knot of worshippers, including my own dear wife, who were still working hard, polishing the floor at midnight ready for the opening ceremony on 4 October 1958.

Chapter Thirteen

Farewells and New Beginnings

After a decade in Rotherham and many intense and challenging experiences both as a co-minister and a solo practitioner I felt it was time to leave for pastures new. My work at Masbro' was done and I was pleased to have seen the developments at Herringthorpe finally come to fruition. After consultation with Dolores, we decided we would take a sabbatical year in Europe while I made up my mind about my post-Rotherham future as a minister. And so, after many tears and protracted farewells from the good people of Masbro' and Herringthorpe, we set sail in early 1959, leaving Hull and heading to Rotterdam. From there we would take trains and buses to wherever our imagination and instinct led us. Luckily, we had the resources to do this; my minister's stipend wasn't much but it kept us alive and so the money Dolores earned we were able to save up. It was this pot of resources we were able to use to finance the sabbatical year.

We had no plan other than to enjoy each other's company away from the pressures of everyday life we had endued for the previous decade. Dolores was, naturally, keen to see as much as possible of Europe and so we visited a selected number of northern and middle European countries, including Holland, Germany and Switzerland, before arriving in Italy.

It was on a train heading south through Italy that we experienced one of those remarkable encounters which stay fixed in the memory forever. We were sharing an apartment with three Italian nuns and

I passed a couple of gentle remarks about them to my wife, safe in the knowledge that they wouldn't understand me.

"Are you enjoying your time in Italy?" asked one of them, in perfect English.

Well, to say that I blushed to my roots is an understatement! However, the nun and her compatriots, who also spoke fine English, were as charming as they could be, and when I introduced myself as a minister – albeit of a faith far removed from that of Roman Catholicism – this temporary friendship was cemented.

They asked us where we were headed. "Rome," I replied.

"Will you see the Pope?" said one of them.

"How does one go about doing that?" I asked, incredulous they should make such a suggestion.

The nun explained that it was possible to obtain tickets for an audience with His Holiness and, once we reached Rome, we were to contact the offices of the American Church there to apply. So, on arrival, that's exactly what we did. "We are not Roman Catholics," I explained to one of the priests at St Susanna, the American Church's headquarters. Laughingly, he replied, "Well, we won't hold that against you." Nor did they, for within a few hours two pink tickets had come from the Vatican authorising our entry to 'Section 30' at St Peter's the following day.

We could not honestly claim to come within the category of those who merit a private audience, people like prime ministers, presidents, and kings. We were not even minor VIPs of the sort who are sometimes taken in by the dozen or the score for a group audience. Indeed our tickets entitled us to see the Pope only at a public audience with about 5,000 other ticket-holders in the nave of the world's largest church. These audiences are held twice a week.

The then-Pope, John XXIII, was due to arrive at 5pm but people began to take up their positions nearly two hours before and at that time we too stood in our allotted place under the great dome of Michelangelo. Wooden barriers divided the vast expanse of the nave into sections, each of which was reserved for some international or local delegation. All had to stand, except the privileged few sitting in boxes built up in tiers round the main pillars, and some children who had seats at the back of the High Altar.

During the long wait I had intended to read the prayers of Dr WE Orchard who was successively a Congregationalist and a Roman Catholic. But the book was never opened, for my attention was gripped by the growing crescendo of colour and activity within the church.

A party of visiting priests entered the adjoining section and ran to the front, jockeying for a place; a hundred or more newly married couples from Germany in full wedding attire came silently down the nave to a special stand at the front; the magenta copes of arriving bishops were outshone by papal chamberlains in buckle shoes.

At the precise moment of his entering, the interior of St Peter's, which had remained dark until now, was suddenly illuminated by thousands of lights and the full scene was revealed in all its magnificence. His Holiness, carried up the nave to the High Altar, smiled as he went and gave the papal blessing. Thousands applauded and cried, "Il Papa! Viva Il Papa!" Many crossed themselves as he passed or dropped to their knees in prayer if there was room.

But all were silent as the Pontiff ascended his throne. A chamberlain began to recite a list of all the special groups of pilgrims present that day including a company of priests' housekeepers from England and a delegation of officers and men from a British naval vessel. Each raised a cheer as it was named.

The Pope delivered a twenty-minute sermon in Italian. He was a rotund little man but intensely animated and vigorous in spite of his seventy-eight years, and had a fine, strong voice. He spoke without notes and with great rapidity and constant gesticulation, sometimes being almost impelled from his seat when emphasising a point. One could have wished for the ability to understand Italian, but some of us who did not had to be content with a whispered and fragmentary translation from those nearby. It seemed that the theme of the sermon was the necessity of carrying one's cross in life with faith and courage as Christ carried His. In any event it was a message of deep personal feeling and not without humorous touches which sent ripples of laugher through the congregation.

Immediately this was finished His Holiness delivered a much shorter address in French following upon which lengthy messages were read on his behalf to the nationals of England, Germany, and Spain, each being different in substance. At the close of brief prayers, and to the accompaniment of further acclaim, Pope John was carried back to the Vatican.

Even for a Protestant, and a Congregationalist at that, it had been a fascinating experience. One thing was certain: John XXIII was not merely an 'interim' Pope, as some supposed he would be carrying on former papal policies as a matter of course, until his death should bring some young and brilliant cardinal into office. Nor was he a tired old man, content with being little more than a figurehead. At that time he had initiated some striking innovations, and with far-sighted shrewdness had called a world ecumenical conference to be held in 1962. This was attended by representatives of those churches outside the Roman communion, who found John XXIII to be a kindly, warm-hearted Christ-loving man displaying a deep affinity with ordinary people, but at the same time a clear-minded, strong-willed prelate who would not compromise in the principles on which his church is based.

After this remarkable experience we travelled to Naples and spent some time there before setting sail for Greece and its attendant islands. I'd studied Greek and Hebrew at Lancashire College, but as I quickly discovered on arrival, my Greek was out of date by around 2,000 years. Nevertheless, we got around and ended up spending three delightful months in that sun-blessed place.

One of the places we visited was Skopelos, an island belonging to the Sporades group in the northern Aegean Sea, very much off the beaten track. Then, it could be reached in twenty-seven hours from Athens by means of train and steamer, via Chalkis and Volos. The island had hundreds of pack mules, thousands of olive trees, about 500 people, one car, and two villages – three and a half hours from each other on horseback. There were about twenty churches, all Greek Orthodox. None of them was large and some are so small as to be little more than a room in a private house hung with one or two icons.

"What time are the services?" we asked. The answer astonished us. "There is only one on Sunday, but it begins at 7am and lasts for three hours." We were also to be startled by the fact that most of the worshippers stand up for it all and the majority are not there at the beginning, but drift in at almost any time until just before the end. So it was without any feeling of guilt, therefore, that as late as 8am we climbed the narrow-stepped streets of Skopelos between the dazzling white-washed houses and crept in the side door of one, a large church. All the Greek churches were built in the Byzantine style – square and squat with a dome in the middle, and their snowy, sun-washed exteriors almost blinded the eye.

The church of St Spyridion in Skopelos proved no exception. The inside however was dim, but gently aglow with rich colour; clusters of candles burned, and their reflected light shone in the silver icons and the brass chandeliers. It touched with deep rose the ancient cabinet inlaid with mother-of-pearl which supported a painting of the Madonna, while the massive rood screen, or Ikonostasion as it is called, closing off the lower end of the church and separating the worshippers from the altar, seemed to be quietly on fire with its predominant reds, gold and multi-coloured pictures of saints.

The long and complicated ritual of the three-hour service, which closely adheres to the liturgy of St John Chrysostom, attempts to re-enact in song, sign, and symbol, the earthly life of Christ. Despite this the service was not easy to follow, and one had to be told for example, that when the priest took off the omophorion – a kind of silk cope – from his shoulders and shook violently over the bread and wine as they lay on the altar, this represented the earthquake which occurred during the crucifixion. Other aspects of the service, particularly those involving the participation of worshippers, remain a vivid memory.

Semi-yashmacked old women encased in black came in and made straight for the portrait of the Madonna which, bending low, they kissed. Then afterwards, taking a brown wax candle, they set it up on the nearest candelabra with twenty or thirty others. In moments of special holiness, as for example, in the Great Entrance of the priest, these same women would kneel down, and in a spirit of keenest worship bend their bodies until they touched the marble floor. The young women, however, were less demonstrative and remained standing throughout in their smart modern clothes.

Although most Greek churches appeared to have no organ, no hymns and no anthems, (and no sermon, except about three times a year on Festival days) the music proceeded non-stop. It was provided by groups of men sat on high chairs near the front of the church who took it in turns to chant the liturgy. Their singing fell very strangely on western ears, slipping as it did with startling rapidity from one key to another and back again, in the manner of oriental music.

While the worshippers were wrapped in continuous devotion, hour after hour, the priest was equally busy. He wore a voluminous white silk robe, red stole, and stove pipe hat, behind which his long hair was knotted into a bun, a compulsory tonsure along with the beard. At Kopelos we entered the church just as the priest, carrying a censor, was threading his way amongst worshippers, and as it swung in their direction, they crossed themselves three times and genuflected. Later on, the scripture was slowly intoned in a high-pitch voice from a vast Bible emblazoned in red and gold.

But all this was preliminary to what was called the Great Entrance. This was when the priest came down into the body of the church bearing in silver vessels the bread and the wine, symbols of Christ's sacrifice. He held them high for the adoration of the people, and they in turn prostrated themselves in silent devotion. He then returned to the altar, which the congregation could just glimpse through the open doors of the Ikonostasion, and closing them behind him partook of the communion solitarily and in silence.

There was no general distribution of the Elements, but members of the church who so desired and if they had previously attended confession, were then helped to a spoonful of mixed bread and wine. Some members communicated once a month, but the majority only two or three times a year. At the Skopelos service it was remarkable to see tiny babies carried up to receive their communion. But then, baptism was regarded as carrying with it the full privileges of membership.

At 10am, when the service ended and our legs would barely support us, we were on the point of sitting down for a rest, when a Greek voice with an American accent suddenly addressed itself to us, "Come on up to the priest and get some God bread." It belonged to a jolly little man who had spent thirty-five years in the States. He urged us to join the queue of people who were waiting to get from the priest cubes of bread, each about one inch square. Upon receipt of it, (this was the Bread of Fellowship) they kissed his hand as a mark of affection and respect for one regarded as the representative of Christ. When our turn came, the jolly little man explained that I too was a 'papas'. The young black-bearded priest gazed at my collar and tie, my clean shaven cheeks and short hair, and looked very puzzled.

"What sort of priest?" he asked.

"Congregationalist," I replied. Still no comprehension. Then he suddenly said, "like Presbyterian?" I nodded. A wide smile of understanding broadened his face and he clutched my hands fervently, "Ah," he exclaimed, "Greek Orthodox same as Presbyterian." I smiled back, but secretly wondered at the strange ramifications of the ecumenical movement.

We then spent some time on Santorini, some sixty miles north of Crete and the only island in the world, apart from Krakatoa in the Pacific, which is known to have exploded. Formerly called Calliste – 'the beautiful' – it once provided a safe and sunny home of the primitive olive-skinned people who lived there. They did not know that beneath their feet a volcano burned. The pressure of unimaginable convulsions deep within the earth pushed it gradually upward until the island's fifty square miles became like the lid of a gigantic pressure cooker – without a safety valve.

About 2,000 BC Santorini blew up. The whole centre of the island exploded and sank below the sea which surged into the six-mile-wide hole. The eruption was so violent that islands distant in the Cyclades were covered with ash and pumice while clouds of dust circled the earth and made sunsets brilliant. Only the circumference of the island was left, with sheer cliffs on the inner side looking down into the terrible void and a rolling sea of unplumbed depths.

Since that time new eruptions have sundered the ring into three, with a gut between each, and the sea bed has continually heaved. In the nineteenth century an island of snow-white marble rose in the lagoon and vanished after some years. During 1866 a large mass of twisted black volcanic rock suddenly appeared in the centre of the lagoon and was given the name of Kaumene Island. It supports no shred of vegetation for the ground is so hot in parts that a cigarette can be lit by being held against it, and the air reeks of sulphurous fumes. The island of Kaumene looks like a heap of coke magnified a thousand times. At any rate, that is what we thought when early one Sunday morning our ship from Athens steamed within the broken ring of islands, thus ending its voyage near the long vanished heart of Santorini.

On the Moskanthe, an antique vessel laid down in 1910, our seventeen-hour voyage had been made hideous for all by constant abdominal convulsions. Not even the Greek naval officer on board was exempt. "I can put up with a ship that rolls and pitches," he said, "but not with one that bounces as well."

All this however, was quickly forgotten as we stood on the deck, horizontal at last, and gaped up at the volcanic cliffs rising rust red above us, almost 1,000 feet sheer from the sea. They were topped by a mass of white buildings which shone in the pale sunshine like icing on a slice of wedding cake.

This town, Thera, was reached by means of a zigzag path of shallow steps running backwards and forwards across the cliff face. Donkeys and their owners waited patiently at the bottom to take visitors up. As only six of us disembarked from the steamer, and there were about a dozen donkeys, fierce competition broke out among the owners as to which of them should take us to the top. I became the victim of a battle royal between two of them who were both equally determined that I should ride on their particular beast. One of these toughs seized my right arm and the other my left, then attempted to drag me in opposite directions, all the time hurling fearful oaths at each other, pausing only now and again to shout unintelligible instructions to me. My wife tried to appear unconcerned while the rest of the natives looked on with detached amusement. I treated the whole thing as a joke, forcing myself to laugh with the rest until pain under the armpits came as a warning that unless something was done, I should soon be torn limb from limb.

Providentially just at that moment a sailor pushed his way through the crowd, thrust my two captors apart and thus restored my power of unfettered choice. There was not much to choose between them, but I settled for the less brutal of the two men, and mounted his beast. My wife was already on another and our luggage on a third. We started up, sitting side saddle.

For some reason the animals refused the middle of the path and kept on veering into the low wall which ran up the side to prevent our plunging into the abyss, so that every few moments my legs were crushed between this wall and the thick rib of wood which encircled the donkey's middle. His owner who walked behind with a whip and was at heart a kind man, did his best to prevent for me these painful collisions by yelling at the animal something which sounded like, "Gelaks, Gelaks, de Navry Narps," – prolonging the 'p's into a great bubbling sound. When this had no effect he would murmur softly into the donkey's ear, "Velaks, Velaks," but that had no effect either. I am told that not even other Greeks know what these mysterious phrases mean – only the donkeys and they keep it to themselves.

After having been relieved of fifteen drachmas apiece, we were at length dumped outside the Atlantic Hotel, a small building of pure white marble put up in 1955. We were surrounded by the stone; it was ethereal, cathedral-like, and trailing plants like lianas of the jungle, dozens of feet long hung down from the dazzling white staircases. The veranda outside our room hung out over the lagoon upon which, far below, there floated the Moskanthe, like a tiny celluloid toy. It also commanded a sweeping view of the whole archipelago of islands. Far away across the blank expanse of water there rose another arc of the drowned volcano's rim, but one could not look for long upon that twisty-cratered coast without a trembling of imagination.

To walk in Thera was to be reminded of life's uncertainty. True, the snowy cupolas of Orthodox churches and the barrel-vaulted rooftops of houses half sunk in the ground for safety, provided a pretty view, but there were extensive ruins to be seen, and there was an eerie silence about the place.

Through the centuries it has not been free for long from tremors and quakes. Kaumene erupted in 1935, and earthquakes destroyed property and life in 1936 and 1955. The last one killed fifty-two and 150 were injured. In the following years about half the population had migrated, perhaps through fear of another, perhaps through experience of poverty or both.

The poverty was unquestionable and partially due to the dryness of the island. There was no natural water anywhere. The drills had gone down as far as 300 feet and failed to find any. In view of the unrestricted use one was allowed in the hotel, it could hardly be supposed that every drop of water on the island had to be brought in by sea at the rate of 750 tons every two days. No wonder there had been times in the past when a family's wealth consisted not in drachmas but in the quantity of water they possessed, and there are those who told you of the occasions when this precious commodity became more costly than wine.

One day we rode a bus, or more correctly the bus – for there was only one – to the southernmost village, Emborion. The island stretched out before us like a heap of dust, culminating in the shapeless eminence of Mt Elias (1,900 feet). On its topmost height was a monastery dedicated to Elijah. The bus lurched and rattled on into the desiccated landscape from which it seemed every vestige of colour had been wrung. Yet not quite, for here and there was a solitary fig tree with its ample green leaves and odd clumps of prickly pear cactus which bore masses of hairy vermilion fruit.

With the help of irrigation, Santorini became an unbroken vineyard in the autumn and the grapes hung in sweet ripe clusters, aromatic as they only can be on volcanic islands. But picking had long finished, and with it the sparse rainfall which is just enough to sustain the vines. Now, in November, they lay coiled like sleeping serpents on the parched ground.

Near Emborion, at the seaside, was the ancient capital city built by the Ptolemies of Egypt within whose jurisdiction the island once lay (third century BC). Since 1895 whole streets had been excavated as well as several temples dedicated to Egyptian gods. There had also come to light a gymnasium, a theatre and a barracks. But 300 years before these remains flourished as a city under the Egyptian yoke, the island people themselves, in obedience to the Delphic Oracle, had crossed into North Africa to found the famous colony of Cyrene.

During the last 200 years these outposts of the Cyclades had variously been under the dominion of Romans, Arabs, Venetians, French, Turks, and for a short spell during the war the Germans and Italians. They were now once more part of the Kingdom of Greece.

At that time in the islands, apart from Greek more people spoke French than any other language and this was the tongue which greeted us at Emborion – a thin scattering of off-white houses on a hill which slopes down to the sea. We carried a letter of introduction to the schoolmaster from his cousin in Athens, once a poor lad in the village, but now a wealthy proprietor of a large hotel. He was 'the local boy made good', who had not forgotten his native place. In the school we were shown with proud affection gifts of books and equipment he had from time to time presented to it.

Our arrival was awkwardly timed, for the postman had just brought in rather a large mail which included the wages of the staff – there were only three. Amusingly enough he remained there until every item had been opened, presumably in the hope that its contents would be shown to him, which they were. After that it seemed to be only fair that the schoolmaster should examine every piece of mail which the postman was in the process of distributing to the village. There was some delay while all this went on but when it was finished and the schoolmaster had paid his pretty young assistant her wages for the week – 100 drachmas – he turned his attention to us and apologized for the delay. A short stocky man in late middle age he wore a threadbare and baggy suit which was badly stained, and shoes on which it had long since been impossible to raise a polish.

But it was not only the schoolmaster who bore the imprint of poverty – the whole school did. In spite of Mr Grivas' gifts, visual aids to teaching were seemingly limited to a few coloured pictures of animals and most of the books were ragged with age. Moreover in the classroom and master's room alike the floor of rough boards was without any covering.

The appearance of the boys, who were all crowded into one room – about fifty of them – was eloquent of a depressed economy. None were dressed in other than grey shirts and short trousers, neatly brushed and clean, but stitched, darned, and patched so extensively that in some cases little of the original garment could have remained. So far as we could see none of them wore shoes or socks, and perhaps never had. It was easy to believe that some of their labouring fathers, oft times unemployed, were finding it difficult to bring up a family on nine drachmas a day.

All the same, as we sat with the schoolmaster in his bare little room, Greek hospitality was lavished upon us. Mystified at first by our arrival, he now beamed pleasure to think we were friends of his cousin and that we deigned to visit so remote and unimportant a place. Refreshments appeared. Two boys of about ten years carried in a tray bearing glass dishes of cherry confiture to be eaten with a spoon. (Did such a luxury ever come their way?) Next there came the traditional non-alcoholic drink of south-eastern Europe – Turkish coffee served in tiny cups and thick as gravy.

Our host followed this up by asking us to go home to dinner with him. It was no use protesting, so off we went along a dusty, twisting path to a house high on the side of the hill. A young man whose eyes ran with trachoma crossed the yard as we entered, carrying a wooden pail of water.

It was a large house for those parts, built as a bungalow round three sides of a square stone yard, and full of decaying Victorian furniture. The schoolmaster's aged mother plied us with confiture again, plus the powerful ouzo – a highly potent spirit distilled from grapes and aniseed, and offered on the slightest provocation to those who travel in Greece. Her senile husband told me he had once been schoolmaster in the village for thirty-five years and that his son, our host, had now held that post for the same length of time.

We all sat down to dinner. The main dish was French beans cooked with tomatoes. To go with this, and for us only, they fried two eggs each. These were luxuries indeed and made us realise with some embarrassment that we were receiving extra-special hospitality. When my wife, gently but firmly, protested that she could only eat one egg, the other was seized and devoured with great relish by the old lady. Wedges of white goat cheese came next, cut from a round hard coil, and then a couple of apples. Our glasses were filled and refilled with the local resinated wine, while throughout the meal a young woman stood by the table ready to cut bread whenever we wanted it. With one hand she held the loaf against her chest and fiercely sawed off great pieces with a carving knife held in the other.

Eventually the time arrived for our departure. We realised that it was not possible to pay these poor people for their spontaneous generosity, and that they would not wish it. But surely there must be some way beyond shaking hands and repeatedly murmuring to make our appreciation tangible. There was. Outside the door two young school boys were playing. Neither had been home to dinner and were apparently waiting in the hope of catching another glimpse of the strange foreign people within. They did not wait in vain and when we came out followed us down the hill-path leading to the road. In response to a gesture from our host, I gave them my case to carry, which they did between them with proud pleasure.

On arriving at the bus stop we sat down at an iron table outside a drinking place. There I attempted to press some drachmas into the hands of the two patched and barefoot boys but amazingly, they refused and with polite but firm finality shoved the money toward me across the table. I could see it was no use persisting so handed it to the schoolmaster, requesting that he buy something for the boys. But he merely shook his head and slipped the coins back into my pocket. "It is not possible for us to accept money from guests," he said with a gentle smile.

Later that week as we strolled across the beaches of jet black sand gathering the pumice which floated in upon the waves, and as we sat in one of the dim, stone-floored cafès of Thera, drinking tea with lemon, our thoughts wandered back to Emborion. And finally, the following Sunday morning when we descended the precipitous zigzag to our ship, and even when someone told us, as it moved slowly out of the lagoon, that a hot spring rose from the abysmal depths and scalded the surface of the sea, we did not enthuse about such things, because our mind's eye gazed upon the schoolmaster in his shabby suit and the barefooted boys smiling and waving as our bus lumbered away.

In all, we stayed in Greece for around three months and had many unusual and evocative experiences such as the ones described above. Then the time came for us to depart and we left this handsome, memorable corner of the Mediterranean at Trieste, catching the Orient

Express which would take us all the way to Paris. From there we went to Dinard, on the northern coast of Brittany, and departed for the Channel Islands. Neither of us had been there and were keen to see this little outpost of Britain so close to France. Jersey was the first destination.

Chapter Fourteen

A New Home

Jersey and Guernsey we found to be most pleasant but even then, in 1959, they were commercialised and full of tourists and people on the make. After two or so weeks there we heard about the island of Alderney and, having listened to the stories of its unspoiled beauty and tranquillity, were determined to go there. One day, when conditions were calm and the sun was out, we set sail from Guernsey on a small ferry and an hour or so later arrived on the little island.

Even before we saw it we said, "This is the place." We had travelled right across Europe and lingered in the most stunning of environments but nothing we'd experienced so far could compare to the wonders of this island. We took a holiday let for a couple of weeks and almost immediately got to know the local people, who could not have been warmer or more welcoming. At the end of the fortnight neither of us had the inclination to return to Jersey, Guernsey or anywhere else, and in total we spent around nine months on Alderney, enjoying every moment.

The only Free Church on the island was a Methodist one and through our attendance we got to know the congregation very well; so well, in fact, that when the minister handed in his letter of retirement I was asked if I wanted the job.

By that time I was forty-one and while I was very tempted by the idea of an island congregation and many more years upon this idyll I had to say 'no'. I didn't feel ready for the quiet life I would have inevitably led. It would have seemed like semi-retirement and, like many big decisions in my life, I felt I was being steered away from such an option and towards something else. So perhaps it came as no surprise when, three weeks after I'd been offered the Alderney job, I received a letter from the Redland Park Church in Bristol, asking me if I was interested in the position of minister there.

Dolores and I discussed the matter. We agreed that no matter how beautiful the island and welcoming the people, to remain there at such a young age would not have been right for either of us. We were in the prime of our lives; reluctantly, perhaps, but with a clear sense of purpose, we decided we would leave the island and settle in Bristol.

And so, in 1960, our sabbatical 'year' that in fact lasted fifteen months came to an end. Our friends on Alderney were very sad to see us leave, understandably, but were cheered when we promised to return. Over the years we kept that promise, spending many wonderful holidays there.

I had mixed feelings about coming back to Bristol. I had left there in 1941, as the Blitz was wreaking havoc across the city and in fact one of its casualties was the original Free Church in Redland, which was destroyed by a German bomb in 1940. The shell of the place just about survived but it was so badly damaged that demolition was the only option. Luckily the church didn't lose its loyal congregation, for it owned rooms nearby and was able to host services while a new church was being built.

Redland Park was, I knew, a large and influential church and I stood in awe of the former minister the Rev Basil Sims. What an illustrious predecessor! "Would I be good enough to follow him?" – was my question. I questioned whether I would fit in, and how I would be able to cope with the demands of such a large congregation. However, the Divine Will – and my experiences at Rotherham – prevailed and I was inducted to the pastorate in March 1961. Even so, Mr Croxton-Smith, the church secretary, spoke a chilling word to me, "It's an impossible job you know," he said.

I soon began to understand why. The church always had a reputation for the spiritual and aesthetic quality of the Sunday services, as well as being honoured for the diversity of its outreach into the civic life in Bristol. This depended to some extent on the leadership of the minister. He was expected to 'get involved'. This was symbolised by the civic service held at the church in 1967, attended by the lord mayor and city dignitaries in all their panoply.

Another major expectation was to conduct two whole Sunday services, morning and evening, with a sermon in each. In addition, I was required to give a children's talk on Sunday morning and conduct a midweek service if possible. In addition, it was expected that I would visit as many members of the congregation as possible and, as mentioned above, become involved in the civic life of the city as a Free Church representative. I served on many bodies and organisations in Bristol, including the Bristol Free Church Council, the Bristol Council of Christian Churches, the Advisory Council for BBC Radio Bristol, the Bishop's Ecumenical Commission Sub-committee and the Bristol Congregational Minister's Fraternal. I was also Free Church chaplain to the university and I founded the first branch of the Samaritans in Bristol, which I will talk about in the next chapter.

Suffice to say that I was very busy indeed. I served as president of the Bristol Free Church Council, which entailed such privileges as dining with the Judges of Assize at the Mansion House (and being served second helpings!). My year of office also involved such functions as opening a new wing at Ham Green Hospital and consecrating, with the bishop, the rebuilt All Saints Church in Pembroke Road. And further, I was asked to conduct annual services for various Bristol benevolent societies and banks.

The university chaplaincy entailed taking services for Free Church students who wished to attend and seeing those students who wished to discuss problems, anxieties, etc. The chaplains of various denominations had to meet regularly to discuss our work and share experiences. On one memorable occasion we were visited by the then

Archbishop of Canterbury, Dr Michael Ramsey – famous for his hearty laugh and eyebrow-twitching.

At a meeting with about 500 of the students, instead of giving an address he invited questions. The first was this, "Your Grace, do you think that religion is now obsolete?" The questioner expected a long and learned answer from Dr Ramsey, but instead of that he merely said, "No. Next question?"

For some years I served on the Congregational Fund Board in London – devoted to the aid of ministers and churches in special need. On the Bristol scene I once took part in a 'clergy crawl' with about fifty others who walked for twelve miles on behalf of Christian Aid. (The fact that I was the only one in shorts got my picture in the local press!)

Incidentally, Bristol was the first city in Britain to establish a local council of churches and ever since that time in 1924 the successive Free Church presidents have been assigned their own special stall in the cathedral – a milestone in ecumenical relationships.

Twice during my ministry at Redland Park the church has been brought under the national spotlight by televised Sunday morning services – by the BBC in 1962 and ITV in 1980. Both of these were watched by several million viewers. It was an honour for the church to be asked to appear on TV and we had to undergo a series of rehearsals before the broadcasts which, in those days, went out live. It certainly put Redland Park on the map and resulted in correspondence from all over the country – including a letter from an elderly lady in Dorset who sent two shillings for the collection.

A very different kind of outreach took place over a period of nine years at Christmas time when on Christmas Day a few of us combined to provide Christmas dinner, tea and afternoon entertainment for about forty people in the neighbourhood who would otherwise have been on their own. For this the firm of Harvey's provided pre-prandial sherry, and a good time was had by all – including the Associate Minister, the Rev James Breslin. He offered to recite a Scottish poem as part of the entertainment. He did so in Gaelic – which nobody understood. I made the mistake of asking him for a translation – which turned out to be a vivid and bloodthirsty account of the Glencoe Massacre.

I was always thinking of ways to expand the church's congregation during the years when religious services of all denominations were far less well attended than they had been for many years. I attribute this partly to the BBC which in the 1960s televised in church time the *Forsyte Saga* in twenty-six episodes, and thus lured away multitudes of worshippers – permanently. One of the ideas I came up with was to give my congregation a whole new and modern way of worshipping, and this involved converting the church's roof space into living quarters. I had the notion – albeit tongue-in-cheek – that Dolores and I would hand back the manse in which we lived and take up residence in the church loft space, which could be converted for our use. To boost congregations I intended to have a hole cut in the floor of the conversion which would lead directly to the church below. By means of a fireman's pole I would slide straight into the pulpit on a Sunday morning and immediately begin the service, to gasps of astonishment from the worshippers. If anything would boost attendance, that would! Needless to say, this far-fetched plan was purely for my own amusement, but just imagine the publicity it would've received!

Falling to earth in the black academic gown I wore may have presented some difficulties. I saved this purely for services and ceremonial occasions, and I never wore a dog collar in my entire ministry. The only time I did so was on the voyage back to England and Rotherham from the United States. We had an enormous amount of luggage and we knew – as did the other passengers – that this was likely to be looked through when we arrived at Southampton. I was told by one of the crew members that if I wore a dog collar I would be passed straight through. So halfway through the voyage I borrowed one and began to wear it. However, I grew tired of it and eventually took it off – and when we arrived in port we were waved through unscathed anyway.

On several occasions I conducted parties of pilgrims to the Middle East, especially to the Holy Land, and two of these missions were for the BBC. The first visit was extremely challenging as I hadn't visited any of this area myself before and so had to do a lot of reading up before we left. However, it went very smoothly and as a result I decided to host several more visits. We visited Israel, Syria, the Lebanon and Palestine, and everywhere we went we received a wonderful reception from the local people. It was on one of these visits that I first met Lady Mary Fuller, who was travelling with her husband. When we arrived home they invited us over for dinner and we were mightily impressed by their lovely house. We became firm friends from then on and over the years she has been a staunch friend. If it wasn't for her this account of my life may never have got off the ground, and I remain immensely grateful to her.

There were many memorable incidents on these trips, including one which occurred in a hotel in Damascus. We had stayed overnight, and in the morning a lady came down for breakfast, complaining bitterly that the only window in her room was on the ceiling.

"No other room has a window this high," she said. "It's a disgrace."

"Well," I said, thinking carefully, "you really ought to be grateful, because of all the members of the party you are the only one who has had an uninterrupted view of Heaven."

Redland Park Church was closely associated with the Redland Teacher Training College nearby and on one occasion the students enlivened the Sunday evening service in such a way that it produced headlines in the local press. The *Western Daily Press* described it thus: 'Fifteen barefoot girls danced to *Beethoven's 7th Symphony* last night. A congregation of over 400 saw them at Redland Park Church interpreting three themes – the need to belong, loving thy neighbour and the growing unity of the church.' Photos appeared in several newspapers.

An even more notable event took place in 1972 following the closure of Highbury Congregational Church in Cotham – the mother church from which Redland Park itself sprang in 1861. No less than forty-six members from Highbury were received into membership at Redland Park – together with another twelve from elsewhere. At the welcoming service I was fortunate in being able to remember the names of each one! It was a memorable occasion too when in October 1972 the Congregational and Presbyterian churches in England and Wales came together to form the United Reformed Church. This was marked by a national television service in Westminster Abbey (at which I was present). Most of the churches involved were able to participate in the Abbey service by having TV sets installed for the occasion.

As to the day-to-day programme of services and activities at Redland Park much could be said and in spite of all the 'extra-curricula' engagements, it was these which rightly occupied much of my time. The church not only functioned on Sundays, but it bustled with life during the week. We had our own large company of Scouts, Cubs and Girls Brigade meeting regularly and crowding in for parade services on special occasions. Other weekly attractions included the Men's Forum, the Women's Hour, Group Six for younger people, the Friendship Club, the Prayer Group and others – all coming within the view of the minister who had his own 'input' into these meetings.

My major responsibility, however, was for the two Sunday services and to these I gave the highest priority. I am glad to say that my sermons at Redland Park were never interrupted by cries of "rubbish, piffle, ridiculous" etc as they once were at another church in the neighbourhood, but I shall never forget a unique happening at one morning service. Sitting in a pew just in front of the pulpit were a mother and her young son, who must have been about six. At one point early on in the service this lad pointed to me and in a loud voice said, "Mamma, is that Jesus?" Possibly it was because of my beard. His mother whispered, "No dear," to which the boy replied, "Let's go home then." They stayed for the rest of the service but were never seen again (by me, that is!).

I remember another occasion when something of a miracle

occurred during the service. My sermon was asking the question, "Who or what is the Devil?" I was apprehensive about how this would be received, especially by an elderly lady who was something of a hard-line fundamentalist. Would she denounce me for my views? However, the lady was quite deaf and could hear nothing without her hearing aid. My apprehension mounted in the hymn before the sermon. But then, during the last verse, she suddenly began to fiddle with the hearing aid, then she took it out and shook it, but to no avail. The battery had run down and consequently she heard nothing of my sermon. On the spur of the moment a quotation from the Psalms sprang to my mind, "This is the Lord's doing and it is marvellous in our eyes."

After each service I was in the habit of going to the main exit door in order to shake hands with those on their way out. On one occasion I did so with a woman who worshipped with us and who, incidentally, belonged to the Aetherius Society. She looked at me stonily and said, "Well. If we can't get anything out of the sermon we can always appreciate the music." I was sorry about the sermon but delighted at her reference to the music. For the whole of my ministry the music at Redland Park was inspirational. There were several reasons for this. The church has one of the finest organs in the West Country – a 4-manual Father Willis rightly seen as the Rolls Royce of organs, with 2,240 pipes. It was played by Mr Stanley Parker, a master musician of consummate skill and sensitivity. In addition the church rejoiced in having a choir of about thirty members. They not only led the hymns superbly but also sang an anthem at both services. More than once I was moved to tears by the music at Redland Park, and more than once there sprang into my mind those immortal words of John Milton:

In service high and anthems clear, as may with sweetness through mine ear
Dissolve me into ecstasies and bring all Heaven before mine eyes.

The whole of my ministry at Redland Park was marvellous for me. Of course I made mistakes, such as when I gave a talk to the children one Sunday morning, assuming it was Mothering Sunday but after a moment or two someone shouted out, "But that was last Sunday." The congregation was always tolerant, understanding and generous. The members never seemed to mind when at various times during my ministry I was away with my wife Dolores, perhaps for three months at a time – doing summer ministries in the US and Hong Kong. I have no doubt that everyone enjoyed hearing sermons from someone else for a change.

What a wonderful privilege it was to work amongst such people as those at Redland Park. Of course, over the years we had our differences, but I can honestly say that never either in deacons/elders meetings, church meetings or elsewhere was there any animosity or ill feeling; and those who knew me then will confirm it. I shall always be grateful for the opportunity of working with such a visionary, supportive and enthusiastic congregation.

This testimony must include a tribute to my wife. It would have been impossible for me to sustain such a long and demanding ministry without her help. We were 'in it together', and Dolores had her own special responsibilities in the life of the church. My hopes and beliefs are still the same as they were when I first stepped inside the door of Redland Park, and here they are briefly as I expressed them in my Induction Statement of March 1961.

"The tenets of our Christian Faith are not the superstitions of a dying age but the enshrinement of truths which have a life and death relevance for this and every day. I see the love of God in Christ for us all, the divine mission of the Church, the sacramental nature of life, the unique revelation of Scripture and the eternal destiny of humankind.

My aim is to be a minister of the Gospel in the Name and through the power of Jesus Christ. I shall not try to please everybody, but I shall try to please God. He asks no more of me and no more of you. We shall worship Him and serve Him together as the years go by, and as a church family we shall become ever more closely knit. Such a task as this we can attempt in complete faith because while we do not know what the future holds – we know who holds the future."

Chapter Fifteen

A Good Samaritan

It was the presence of the then Bishop of Bristol, Oliver Tomkins, at my induction ceremony at Redland Park which led to the formation of the first branch of the Samaritans in Bristol. As you may know, the Samaritans organisation was founded by the Rev Chad Varah in London in 1953, having taken the funeral service of a fourteen year old who had committed suicide after she started her periods and having no-one to discuss it with. He was to establish the first Samaritans at St Stephen Walbrook in London, and today there are hundreds of branches across the UK taking many millions of calls and receiving thousands of visitors.

Following my induction I became friendly with Oliver Tomkins and in 1962, a year after I arrived at Redland Park, he asked me, with five others, to meet up with the aim of discussing a Samaritans branch for Bristol. This we did, and during the meeting the bishop told us that Bristol was one of the few big cities left in the country without a Samaritans presence. Obviously, that situation could not last for much longer and there was a real necessity for a branch in the city.

Oliver Tomkins was a compelling and persuasive speaker. When he had finished he looked round at us all – churchmen, legal people and the rest – and simply said, "Well, over to you."

His statement was met with silence. Knowing what a task it would be, nobody wanted to take the initiative. I happened to be sitting next to him, so he turned to me and said, "Now Cyril, would you be willing just to convene the next meeting of this group?" Well, I could hardly say no, so I said 'yes', and a date was fixed for the next meeting of our little group. As we left, I fell in with a Church of England clergyman and we walked up the street together. As we chatted, I said, "I hope you can make the next meeting?"

"Oh no," he replied, "I'm booked to see someone important that day. I'll be there next time." And we never saw him again!

Absentees notwithstanding, the next meeting did go ahead and the whole thing started from there. I was aware that it would be an uphill task to find volunteers, funds and premises but nonetheless there was a deep need for the Samaritans in Bristol and in spite of all the church work I was obliged to undertake I knew it was important to make room for this organisation in my life.

Luckily, I was able to find people who saw merit in the Samaritans and I invited Rev Chad Varah to Bristol several times to speak to different groups and organisations and thus provide inspiration and motivation. After a year's hard canvassing and persuasion we opened the first Bristol branch in June 1964, at 8, St Nicholas Street. We had two rooms and one gas ring but from the beginning we were able to provide twenty-four-hour cover, 365 days in the year, with the help of more than fifty volunteers. As is usual with all Samaritans volunteers I only used my first name followed by a number, and so I became Cyril 001 – the first volunteer in Bristol. The opening of the branch was big news. The HTV organisation (now ITV West) covered it, and they filmed the Lord Mayor of Bristol making the first call. Not that he needed anything, other than to be in the news!

We all had to have intensive training to be able to deal with the range of callers who contacted us. And what a range it was. Even after the first week we realised how badly-needed this service was in Bristol. The Clifton Suspension Bridge, one of the city's most famous landmarks, was (and sometimes still is) a notorious suicide spot and we came to an arrangement that whenever the bridge-keeper saw someone acting suspiciously on the bridge he would have a talk to them and, if it was appropriate, would then contact us and have the person brought to our offices by taxi. Even today, the phone number of the Samaritans is fixed to a plaque on the bridge's famous support structures.

From St Nicholas Street we moved to 1, Unity Street in 1975, but had outgrown this by the following year. Such was the demand for our services that we had to hold meetings with clients on College Green, the Lord Mayor's Chapel, on the stairs and even the kitchen. Finally, we moved to the top two floors of 37, St Nicholas Street. We were offered the whole building for £32,000 but could not afford it at the time. Eventually we did acquire the building for £132,000 and let the ground floor to the Europa Restaurant, which brought in over £20,000 a year in rent. The premises comprised an operations room with three telephones, two interview rooms, kitchen, general office, director's office, two bedrooms, bathroom and shower room, a lounge, and two outsize rooms for training volunteers.

Today, the Samaritans in Bristol take about 36,000 calls a year and have 160 volunteers covering the phones for twenty-four hours, seven days a week. They encourage face to face meetings for clients and they deal with every conceivable kind of human dilemma from broken relations to students' concerned about their exams and various traumas. The Samaritans is entirely funded from private donations with no salaries being paid except expenses, which in practice are hardly ever claimed. The Bristol office is covered by volunteers, who work in three-to-four hourly shifts; 7.30–10.30, 10.30–2pm, 2–6pm, 6–10pm, 10–2.30am and 2.30–7.30am. There are bedrooms available for those on the night shifts.

We have to deal with all sorts of problems from ill health, marriage breakdown, alcoholism, rape and sexual abuse to just about every kind of unimaginable kind of human crisis. We seek to identify ourselves with the caller, providing one hundred per cent confidentiality, never being judgemental or platitudinous. We can never provide any money to help with their problems but can offer a listening ear for as long as it takes. Listening creatively, sensing the implication of what is being said and shaping our response accordingly. We cannot offer to solve their problems for them but we can offer to hold their hand and see them through their darkest hour.

For some of our callers we are the only people in their world who will do that. We can put them in touch with Alcoholics Anonymous, Gamblers Anonymous, Shoplifters Anonymous, a rape line, Child Line, Battered Wives Centre and others. We liaise with doctors, psychiatrists, the clergy and many other specialists in specific areas.

Once a month we have a psychiatrist who comes into the centre to give advice to volunteers dealing with difficult cases. We regularly visit prisons to help prisoners and train prisoners to help their fellow inmates twenty-four hours a day.

What sort of people are the volunteers? They must not be judgemental, censorious, patronising or shockable and they must have the ability to listen and go on listening and have genuine concern for the callers' well-being. They must have the sense to realise that if confidentiality is breached the whole of Samaritans is compromised. Above all the volunteers need enough coolness and stamina to deal with concentrated misery and not be overwhelmed by it.

The busiest time for Samaritans is between 10.30pm and 2am. We receive no statutory funding and rely on voluntary contributions. We also provide an email system of help – some enquiries come from as far away as the United States.

Of course, there are unanticipated bonuses. The formation of long-lasting friendships and partnerships as well as free gifts from the corporate sector like Tetley's tea bags, chocolate from Cadburys, and sherry from Harvey's are just some of those. One supporter provides a flower arrangement for the reception area every two weeks and no-one knows who the donor is! One lady called with a brown paper bag containing £500, saying how grateful she was to the Samaritans for saving her son's life.

Behind the 36,000 calls a year there are chasms of grief, oceans of emptiness and universes of pain. Sometimes you are so moved that you want to envelop the person in your arms and give them all the time you've got and all that you are. But then you come down to earth and in the words of Chad Varah, "If they ring and find a friend what we offer is not a placebo but something as basic as bread." I take the view that if we are able – even just a little – to reduce the sum total of human misery we should feel privileged to have had just a small share in that.

I stayed as a volunteer for fifty years, long after I retired from the ministry. In April 2012 I received the Lord Mayor's medal for my services to the organisation and in July of that year I received a letter from the Queen, letting me know that I was to receive the MBE for the same work. I'm not sure who recommended me – though I have a very good idea! – and later that year I was due at Buckingham Palace to collect the honour. However, shortly before the ceremony we were informed that the location had changed to Windsor Castle and the Princess Royal was to preside over the ceremony. That was no disappointment to me. She is a very nice lady and I was delighted to have the chance to see Windsor Castle. When we arrived I saw a piano in one corner of the room and, being a lifelong musician, just like my father, took an obvious interest in it. One of the ceremonial attendants said that I could try it out of I liked, so I had a little tinker on the keys. It was a lovely instrument. The ceremony was very pleasant and I chatted to the Princess Royal for a while about the work of the Samaritans. After it was over we went into Windsor for lunch and it was there, to my surprise and delight, that I met my step-nieces; Susan, Barbara and Janet. As I've said before, they are a delight to me.

One of my Bristol Samaritan friends, Maggie 20, has been asked to write a piece for inclusion in this book, and I'm pleased to be able to reproduce it below. She has spoken very kindly of me, but that aside I hope it gives some insight into the wonderful work that all the Samaritans in Bristol, and across the world, do every day of the year.

The Rev Cyril Grant was asked in 1963 to establish a branch of the Samaritans in Bristol and he readily took on this challenge. His foresight and vision of wanting to offer this service was very pioneering at this time of 'cultural hostility' of the early 1960s. Working closely with Chad Varah he assembled a group of people and provided the inspiration and drive to make sure that the project was taken through to its successful conclusion, opening in 1964. He became the Chair of the Trustees of Bristol Samaritans and remained so until 1982. Thus began the Samaritan career of Cyril 001.

He retired in his fiftieth year of service. During those years he fulfilled many roles, including serving as Director, Chair, Leader and throughout as an ordinary volunteer.

I arrived as a rookie volunteer in 1978 and met Cyril very soon after my training. This wonderfully sprightly man, with his dapper appearance in a suit with a wonderfully foppish pocket handkerchief and sporting a 'Colonel Sanders' beard, caught my attention. With the twinkle in his eye and wonderful sense of humour, he made me feel very at home in the organisation. He was an inspiration to observe when taking calls and we all learned from him. The support we received from him was invaluable and he helped us all to be more confident in developing our listening and responding skills, thus influencing our development hugely. What an influence to exert and for us to have experienced!

Cyril is able to be all things to all men. Simply, he likes people. He set us all an example of giving selflessly to our callers; never being pious, but accepting everyone unconditionally and on their terms. At the same time, he is a man of dignity and integrity who, I feel, has no sense of his own brilliance or of the profound impact that he has had on the lives of so many (volunteers, callers and friends) for so long.

He also has the gift of making life-long friends and of

making them all feel very special to him. Each of us feels treasured and my own friendship with him spans thirty-five years.

Friends might be introduced to new things, such as to the jazz in 'The Old Duke' (very loud, but he loved it), taken for lunches in 'Berni Inns' or in various ethnic restaurants. Throughout, we would be talking and talking incessantly, with Cyril telling of his and Dolores' amazing exploits and one was always spellbound. His quixotic humour, vast vocabulary and love of words is always so stimulating. However it was never all one way. He has such a gift of making us feel that we are important. He was genuinely interested in our lives. He enjoyed hearing of our exploits and made us feel very special.

If ever we were in any trouble, he would be there for us in every way. He also loved to share in our happiness and was genuinely moved by being involved in my marriage ceremony.

Cyril's huge sense of fun knows no bounds. We have photos of him dressed and made-up as a 'wench' and all sorts of other fancy dress. I have a movie of him spontaneously bursting loudly into song on a promenade, 'Oh, Lucky Jim...' to the amazement and joy of passers by.

Cyril has given talks to many groups of people, but on such diverse topics; not the sort that you would expect from a minister of religion. The audience listened with glee to his talk on 'My Hats', of which he had over sixty, many of which were worn as visual aids! Another favourite to hear was 'My Failings', which always had an audience in stitches. When, years later, it was my turn to give talks and Cyril was in the audience, he would be in the front row and beaming at me. That was so affirming and such a joy!

It is my privilege to say that this is my friend, Cyril 001, who has shared in and shaped so much of my life.

Maggie 20, Bristol Samaritans

Chapter Sixteen

Retirement and Beyond

With a heavy heart I decided to retire from my ministry at Redland Park in 1984. I was sixty-five, and sad to leave my beloved flock after twenty-four years, but at the same time it was exhilarating to contemplate the possibilities of an unfolding future. I admit to a feeling of relief that I would no longer have to prepare for two services for every Sunday as well as a children's address. Moreover I was a part-time chaplain at the University of Bristol.

Of course, we had to leave the manse and find somewhere else to live. Neither Dolores nor I had ever owned any property and the manse, which had been our home, belonged to the church and would be needed for the next minister. Fortunately the United Reformed Church Retired Ministers Association came to our aid and a house was purchased for us in the Horfield area of Bristol and for which we paid a very reasonable rent.

Then it was necessary to transfer our church membership to another congregation for the reason that it is regarded as professionally unacceptable to remain in the same church after the appointment of a new minister; and that is very understandable. We happily became members of the Henleaze URC – a church which I have known since the mid 1930s.

With more time on my hands than before I was able to extend my work for the Bristol branch of the Samaritans (of which I was the only founder member left). Apart from telephone duties at the headquarters in St Nicholas Street I was able to give more talks to various bodies on how we seek to help the distressed and suicidal. I also expanded my repertoire by including in it such subjects as 'Ecclesiastica Fantastica' and 'My Failures' – outlandish, but also humorous. My experiences in such countries as Australia, China, the USA, Africa, Europe and the Middle East were offered as the subject of talks.

When it comes to 'My Failures', people often wonder why a man of religion should actually admit to such failures at all. But failure, as well as success, is an excellent measure of the human condition. To be unable to admit to failure is to deny yourself a great deal of insight and wisdom and, as Winston Churchill said, "Those who do not understand the lessons of history are forced to repeat them." So I think it is vital that I not only acknowledge my failures, but talk about them in a humorous way. Below are just a few examples:

I have known my great friend, John Funnell (who has worked so painstakingly on this book) since 1962. He has been married twice and I officiated at both his weddings. He was married first at Amersham Free Church in 1967, in a double wedding that included his sister and her husband-to-be. During the service I got slightly confused and almost married John off to his sister! John's father, a dear friend of mine, who was 'giving away' his daughter, stopped me from making a major bloomer.

I remember the occasion when I caused a major marital rift with some newlyweds where the wife discovered on their honeymoon that I had dated the marriage certificate a week later so they weren't officially married, which nearly ended the marriage before it had started. I also double booked a wedding at the same time for two different couples, who had both printed their orders of service for the wedding. Not knowing how I could solve this dilemma I was very relieved when one of the prospective wives phoned me in great dismay to say that she and her betrothed had had second thoughts and how very sorry she was for all the inconvenience.

On another occasion I was stopped by my deacon, Arthur Bodey, who removed six spoons from my waistcoat which I'd accidentally placed there while helping at a wedding reception held at a nearby hotel. Another time, I realised that I did not have a bride's father's name as I was completing the register so I thought I'd better ask her mother. Her reply astonished me. "I never found out," she said.

I know I've made many more gaffs over the years but as age advances my memory isn't as good as it was, so there are rather convenient gaps in my knowledge. However, I wasn't always a failure as my first word was not Mamma or Dada, but phospherine. And it was all downhill from there!

As well as such talks and the Samaritans work, retirement brought with it the chance to spend more time in the garden, and how relaxing this was! In addition to flowers we grew kidney beans, potatoes, courgettes, marrows, spinach etc plus tomatoes in the greenhouse. We also had many wonderful holidays and returned to Alderney time and time again. We never regretted not settling there but we were always pleased to return to the warm welcome we'd enjoyed for many years.

On that note, one of the biggest bonuses of retirement was that Dolores and I had more opportunity to be together and do things together. We both learned to drive after I retired, never previously having been behind the wheel of a vehicle in our lives. We found this to be a great benefit, and it brought back childhood memories of travelling in my father's car as a small child. He had a big old thing, made in 1909, and the only brake was on the outside so that if you wanted to stop you had to reach out of the vehicle and pull it back. There was but room for two in the front and on the back, outside of the car, was a 'dickie seat'. I was placed on this when my parents went out for a drive and it was a miracle that I was still with them when they reached their destination!

The time I had with Dolores was a great joy. Sadly, she died in 2007 thus bringing to an end our happy marriage of 59 years. I was shattered by the loss and attending her funeral was one of the hardest things I've ever had to do. It was at the church we belonged to in

Henleaze, Bristol, but I did not officiate at it.

Now I have to look after myself and do most of the domestic chores; but thankfully I was initiated into all this eighty years ago by my step-mother who dragooned me into doing all kinds of household duties – which I then resented – but which now I am thankful for being able to do.

I'm now in my nineties, of course, and not quite able to do all the things I used to do, but I thank God that I am able to live a full, enjoyable and hopefully useful life without the help – so far – of spectacles, false teeth, hearing aid, a walking stick, or a stair-lift. And, remarkably, perhaps, I still sport my trademark beard, which I feel I must say something about. It has been a constant companion for more than seventy years and, like a faithful dog, deserves some acknowledgement in these pages.

My facial hair made its first appearance in the Second World War. "There's nothing for it," said the college doctor, "you'll have to grow a beard," thus ending my weary battle with the youthful complaint of acne vulgaris, popularly called pimples. They covered my face and I could never shave without opening them; the result can be imagined. All kinds of remedies were suggested to me, and once I went about every day for months with a face smeared with sulphurous-smelling liquid. But it was no good.

So I was relieved to hear the doctor's desperate suggestion. No one enjoys carrying his visage before the world when it resembles a mass of multicoloured nodules. But now things were to be different, and instead of being revolted, I could look forward to the time when people were going to admire a facial covering of which any man would be proud.

The beard was begun and it had immediate practical advantages; the saving of time, torment, nervous energy, and cash. After about a week, short thick stubble made an even growth over the lower cheeks, jaws and chin, but with the peculiarity that it was black everywhere except on the chin, and just there it came out in a distinctive auburn tint. Later on, in order to appear less conspicuous I dyed this part the same colour as the rest.

During the three or four weeks that the beard was in process of growing, the hard bristles caused a prickly sensation which made me want to tear my face to shreds, but this disappeared when the hairs grew long and bushy.

At last the day came when I began to look like an Old Testament patriarch. And at first I spent much time before the mirror admiring and stroking this remarkable growth. The nodules soon subsided and at the same time lost their kaleidoscopic hues. I wondered, and still do, why the majority of males endure so much anguish and trouble every day to frustrate the wise designs of nature.

In a decade when almost no one sported a beard except professors, naval commanders and eccentrics, I was sometimes mistaken for all three. On one occasion, when, as a normal and soberly dressed human being, I was walking in the same direction as the university students rag procession, I must have got too near to it, and was mistaken for one of the participants, receiving loud applause.

Another day, while I was walking down Market Street in Manchester, a man suddenly jabbed me in the stomach, shouted, "Beaver," and disappeared before I could think of a suitable reply.

Though a mere undergraduate, I was more than once mistaken for a professor, and only very recently there passed from mortal life the Dean of Faculty who once went out of his way to accost me at a university function. He shook my hand vigorously, smiled benignly and spoke to me as an intimate until being made aware of the fact that I was still struggling to pass the Intermediate degree examinations in his own department.

But sometimes it turns out that this possession of a beard is indeed the passport to privilege. This happened once when I was on a crowded train going to London. The journey had just begun, and hundreds of people were having to stand in the corridor. The ticket inspector could hardly get through, and after examining my ticket, he looked at me twice and then said in a half whisper, "Would you care for a seat, sir?" I knew that every compartment was jammed, and could not imagine where he was going to put me, but on the other hand, I did not look forward to standing up for the next four hours. So, without asking any awkward questions, I said, "Yes, please."

"Follow me," he replied. We eventually pushed our way through to the guard's van, and there I felt able to breathe. With perfect courtesy, he ushered me into the solitary well-cushioned arm chair reserved for the guard, and said, "I hope you will be comfortable there, sir." I was, for the rest of the ride to London.

Such things would not have happened unless I had learned one of the primary lessons of beard-possession, namely that regular trimming is essential if they are to attract rather than repel.

Mine used to be done by a local barber called Alfie. He was a shrivelled little man, who recalled with misty eye the days when long ago he clipped twenty or thirty beards a day. Now they were all gone, and mine was the first he had had for years. Its luxuriant growth was the pride and joy of his circumscribed life. Every time I went in, he trembled with emotion, and snipped away with such shaking fingers that by way of self-protection I would be compelled to say, "Not too short, please." My appearance once a week caused the flame of professional pride to leap into the old man's heart. I was in the chair twice as long as anybody else because he spent so much time standing back to admire the work – like a Michelangelo surveying his David. It was almost with an embarrassed apology that he took from me the nominal charge of three pence, and I sensed he was hardly able to bear the intrusion of so sordid a necessity into the pure practice of his art.

But three years after my visit to the doctor, this whole business of beard wearing and trimming came to a sudden end. One morning news arrived that I had been awarded a Travelling Fellowship in the USA, and the authorities insisted that I must go clean-shaven. It was useless to protest; they had their own reasons and held all the strings, so I went to Alfie, and said, "Cut it off." I was always pulling his leg and he laughed very much at this little sally. After a few moments however, he saw that I was in earnest and the poor old man nearly broke down. I told him what had happened, and after partially recovering from the shock, without another word he braced himself, and seizing a cutthroat took the beard off in one great piece like rind from cheese.

As a concession to his feelings, I promised to take the beard home and keep it in a large envelope so that I could be reminded of happy hours in the chair. I meant this to be taken as a joke, but Alfie thought it was a serious suggestion and packed the beard for me in a brown paper bag – after first removing his lunch from it.

Some months afterwards, when I was in America, news came that within a few weeks of my last visit, the little barber had given up his shop and died. Some years later, while clearing out the attic at home, I was reminded of all this by a bulging brown paper bag. There was the beard – as black and wiry as the day it was cut off. On the spot I decided to grow another, and I hope that wherever Alfie is, he sees and is happy.

Chapter Seventeen

Giving Thanks

It is with a heavy heart that I arrive at the final chapter in my autobiography, and if you have stayed with me all the way I can only thank you for your tolerance and saint-like patience! I have had a long and largely happy life, which I hope has come across clearly through the narrative, and since my vocation became clear all those years ago I have been humbled and honoured by the many people I have met and ministered to. You are all in my thoughts, each and every one of you.

I always enjoyed writing and, as I mentioned, I had intentions of a career in journalism. Had it not been for a confidence-sapping interview with the then-editor of the *Bristol Evening Post* in the 1930s, I should've been very pleased to don a mackintosh and reporter's trilby hat and pound the streets in search of news stories. But it wasn't to be, and when I look back I see that God had other plans for me. I've never once questioned my vocation; it may be that I've met even more people than I might have done as a journalist and I'm not at all sure that journalism – especially the modern variety – could really have counted as 'God's work'! So I believe Divine Intervention has shaped my life and when I have had an important decision to make, or had to choose between diverging paths, I've always felt that Divine Intervention has been my ultimate guide.

That said, there have been occasions when I've been unsure of the Spirit's intentions. In the bad winter of 2011 I went to my Co-op for some bananas but they did not have any so I left feeling rather despondent. Crossing the road I had to stop on the central island to let cars pass and saw some yellow in the snow, which when I scraped the snow away revealed three perfect bananas.

"Yes," I thought, "Divine Intervention is at work once more."

However, as I attempted to pick them up I slipped and fell. A passer-by tried to help me up, only to fall as well. This caused the traffic to come to a halt while people came to the rescue and helped my helper and me to our feet. Feeling a little dazed I returned home to realise that I had lost my keys, without which I could not get in; so I walked back up the road and crossed to the middle and found them there in the snow where I had fallen!

Talking of the Co-op and icy conditions, that story reminds me of another occasion I set out to do my shop in cold weather. I like to wear shorts, even on cold days, and on this occasion I went out in them, perhaps ill-advisedly. A passer-by stopped in their car and the lady passenger enquired why I was dressed in these shorts in Icelandic conditions. I replied, "I am doing it to repent all of my sins, of which there are many," to which she replied. "Oh, I am sorry!"

As I say, I have had many happy times in my life, the happiest of which I spent with Dolores, my dear late wife. We didn't have a family, which is a regret, but it just didn't happen for us and so instead we led a full and busy life, which included a great deal of travelling. Perhaps we would not have seen so much of the world had we had children, but a family would have been a source of great pleasure to us and I'm sorry it didn't happen. However, I cannot complain; for sixty years I had a wonderful relationship with Dolores and we were everything to each other. She even liked Rotherham and found the differences between her new life in England and her previous existence in the USA more intriguing than frustrating. I remember her going into a grocer's shop one day and asking for twenty-seven cookies, only to find they had no idea what she meant. She gained secretarial work at Steel, Peach and Tozer's steel works, having to borrow a pair of shoes to wear to the interview because money was in short supply. Later she became a teacher at the local junior school. She became president of the local Soroptomists club, and throughout the ten years in the town she unstintingly supported me in the growing ministry at Masboro' and Herringthorpe.

The fact is that in those days Rotherham with its innumerable adjacent coal mines, steel works and other heavy industries was one of the grimiest and polluted towns in the country. When Dolores saw it, with the clutter of tiny back to back houses with their back yards and out-door toilets, she described it as 'quaint'.

She began teaching when Elvis Presley was the dominant figure in the world pop music scene. Children and young people were obsessed with him. This became evident when one day in class Dolores put this series of questions to the children:

Q: Who is the greatest man in the world?
A: Elvis Presley
Q: What is your idea of happiness?
A: To be married to Elvis Presley
Q: What is the greatest privilege that could ever come to you?
A: To be allowed to die for Elvis

Dolores supported me in my Ministry, using her secretarial skills in administration, pastoral skills in visiting, and her generous gifts of welcoming and entertaining. She was a good cook and around the food she prepared many had been made to feel at home. As I've said, she often accompanied me with the parties I took to the Middle East. We did several pastorate exchanges in the United States where she took the opportunity to see family, and together we went to Hong Kong, after which we took the opportunity to see some of China, travelling 3,000 miles by public transport in our independent explorations. In all of these travels we made new friends from all over the world.

During our Rotherham ministry there lived with us a series of theological students who, in turn, spent a period of six months working alongside me in order to gain practical experience of church and ministerial life before they embarked upon it themselves.

At one period we agreed to give accommodation to a young woman from Ghana who was coming to England to be trained in Housing Management – with the prospect of becoming the first European-trained housing manager the Ghanaian government would ever have had.

She resided with us for two years. Her name was Amy Ofiri and her father was a bishop of the Anglican Church in Ghana. She proved to be a most intelligent and charming guest – always eager to help Dolores with the domestic chores. However, during her long stay there occurred a unique incident. One morning she fell from the top to the bottom of the stairs and crashed into our antique grandfather clock which had belonged to our forebears. It was smashed to pieces by the impact, but she suffered only minor injuries.

We made our claim on our insurance company for the loss of that time-piece – but the imperious company turned it down on the grounds that our policy did not cover any damage that might be done by 'black girls falling into grandfather clocks' – their words. However, there was one unexpected compensation; when some years later Amy became married, the name they gave to their first born was – CYRIL!

This reminds me of the time a couple asked me if I would christen their child and I asked what name they wished to call him but they did not know and asked me for a suggestion. I thought for a moment and then suggested Basil and they agreed that this should be his name. On another occasion I agreed to christen my niece's son. They wanted my suggestions, but it had to be biblical, so I suggested Potiphar. This was not what she had in mind and most sensibly chose to call him Matthew instead.

I have always tried to look on the bright side of things, and retain a sense of humour about life. Perhaps this has made me something of an unconventional clergyman, but there are times when having a sense of humour is the only thing that will comfort you and see you through the difficulties of life. The treatment my stepmother meted out to me as a boy may have removed my sense of humour forever but I fought hard for this not to happen and it didn't. In fact, I look at it now as a positive; it helped me empathise with people who were having a hard time of things and it made me realise that no-one is perfect, not least myself.

You may be wondering why the front cover of this book depicts me in a Scottish Tam o'Shanter hat. My surname is Scots but I have no connections with Scotland and have never even been there. The fact is, I've always had a 'thing' about hats and it so happened I was wearing my Tam o'Shanter when my friend John Funnell's wife Gay created a pastel drawing of me in 1989, which now hangs in my hall. I have given talks about my hats on various occasions and below are the 'explanations' for just some of the hats I've owned:

1 CAP. As some geriatric patients at Manor Park Hospital said when they saw me, "Why, it's dear old Edward VII come back to us again."

2 LARGE TOPPER. I would not have bothered to replace it if it were not for my frequent invitations to Buckingham Palace Garden Parties.

3 CARDBOARD POINTED. This is the hat that best fits my personality.

4 OLD TRILBY. This is for less formal occasions such as digging the garden. It is a hat of 1956 vintage whose brims were distorted by the great Rotherham floods of that year.

5 BLACK STETSON. This one I bought in El Paso, Texas. I chose black so that I could wear it at funerals without being conspicuous.

And so on!

To conclude, I feel the world today is a better place than the one I was born into. There are more opportunities for people and life is richer than it was. Of course, there is still much work to be done before all of humanity achieves equal rights, freedom from want, political stability and a decent standard of living, among many other things. There is also the question of religion; when I was a boy, the churches I attended were packed to the rafters. Today, they are far from that and congregations are dwindling year by year. As a minister who tried his best to encourage people to go to church I find this sad. But perhaps I am not so disheartened as I should be because I believe that 'what comes around goes around' and I feel there will be a resurgence of religious interest in years to come. Where there is a need – and there is always a need – there will be a place for churches and church men and women.

I will end where I began, back at my first school in Sparkbrook, Birmingham. One of my schoolmasters wrote the following lines in my copybook and I've never forgotten them. They have been instructive words all my life, and I hope they may give you, my dear reader, some inspiration too:

Don't look for the faults as you go through life.
And even if you find 'em,
'Tis wise and kind to be somewhat blind,
And look for the virtues behind 'em.

Cyril H Grant, September 2013